Decorating Pottery

with Clay, Slip and Glaze

by F. Carlton Ball

A Ceramics Monthly Magazine Handbook
WILLIAM C. HUNT, Editor
MARK MECKLENBORG, Publisher
ROBERT L. CREAGER, Art Director

THE AMERICAN CERAMIC SOCIETY
Westerville, Ohio

ACKNOWLEDGMENTS

The author wishes to express his appreciation to his Graduate Assistants, Bob Held, and Huey Becham, and to the other Graduate students for their encouragement and help. He is especially indebted to Sam Calder, a professional photographer and potter, for his assistance in preparing material for this book.

 The American Ceramic Society
735 Ceramic Place
Westerville, Ohio 43081

04 03 02 01 00   26 25 24 23 22

ISBN: 0-934706-05-0
Library of Congress Catalog Card Number: 67-19833

Visit: www.ceramics.org
             www.ceramicsmonthly.org
             www.potterymaking.org

Table of Contents

Foreword

THERE ARE INNUMERABLE TECHNIQUES for decorating pottery. The ones presented in this handbook are intended for use by those potters, either beginning or advanced, who want to explore the possibilities of surface enrichment but lack skill or confidence in drawing and painting. These methods were especially devised for such persons in order to give them some simple means of decorating with clay, slip and glaze. They are techniques that any potter can use easily and effectively, whether or not he is proficient with a pencil and brush. Because each one involves a single principle of working, they might be called "pure techniques." If a ceramist first becomes familiar with each of these, later on he can experiment in combining them and thus develop his own individual style of decorating.

Many of the decorating methods introduced here are closely associated with the regular processes of making and glazing pottery. Finger or tool marks left in the clay from throwing on the wheel, coil building, or paddling a pot into shape are basic elements of decorating that may be used just as they are, or accented with slip or glaze. If the craftsman sponges or sands away these finger or tool marks, he may destroy much or all of the pot's character and beauty. If the potter applies glaze to a pot by dipping or pouring, this in itself may create a handsome and satisfying decoration; however, if he paints glaze on a pot to make it *appear* dipped or poured, there is every chance that the effect will be artificial and unsatisfying.

The first six projects in this book are concerned with the manipulation or addition of clay for decoration while the pot is in the formative stages; the next seven projects involve the use of slips or engobes for surface enrichment on greenware; and the last seven projects have to do with the selection of glazes and their use for decorative effects on bisque ware. Finally there is a section devoted to slips and engobes and another that lists the glaze recipes mentioned in the text and captions.

It would take several lifetimes to explore all of the possible variations and combinations of these decorating techniques. The potter always has something new to investigate; he always will. This certainly is a large part of the fascination of working with clay, slip and glaze.

F. Carlton Ball

Altering Basic Shapes

Far left: Protruding ridges were formed by pressing out and up with a finger from inside. Round dimples were made by pressing against the clay from the outside with the finger.

Left: The clay was pushed outward from the inside with the index finger to form lumps or bumps for a decorative effect. G-Matt-3 Green-Brown glaze, Cone 10 reduction.

WHEN A POTTER has made an attractive form, either by throwing on the wheel or hand building, he hesitates to change its shape. However, he can give the piece a very special decorative character by using his fingers to press the clay in or out to alter the original form. The potter's own fingers are his most important tools and he should not overlook their use in exploring the possibilities of decoration.

After the pot has been formed, and while it still is on the wheel, the clay is soft and pliable enough to be manipulated easily. Even if the pot is allowed to stand until the clay becomes somewhat stiffer, the form still can be altered with the fingers; however, the character of the decoration will be different because of the stiffer condition of the clay.

A first exercise in deforming a soft clay pot might consist of using a finger inside the pot to push up and out against the wall to form a protruding ridge. A series of these ridges can be used to change the basic round shape into one with four, five or six sides. Additional decoration can be added by pushing with the finger against the clay wall from the outside to form round dents or dimples. Vertical series of these dimples might be used alternately with the protruding ridges to create a pleasing decorative effect.

A reverse form of the round indentations can be used effectively as the sole decoration of a vase. A single finger is used from the inside to push the clay outward into lumps or bumps. These may be in a regular or random pattern, and they may all be of one size or alternate between large and small ones. If the bumps on the surface are rather bold ones, it is best to start with a thicker-walled pot. If the wall is thin, there is some danger that it may collapse or that the clay may split when it is forced too far by the finger. A means of successfully stretching thin clay is to push it out into just a small bump, then take a flattened marble or pellet of clay and apply this to the inside indentation to act as filler clay. This clay patch allows the potter to stretch the wall without danger of splitting it. An interesting variation of this method consists of holding a small concave mold on the outside wall, then pushing the clay from inside to fill the mold. This results in a series of very regular round ridges.

A more elaborate decorative effect can be made by working with a tall cylinder and altering it to create a lobed vase that would be excellent for flower arrangements.

1. The index finger is pushed into the soft clay at the base of a cylinder and drawn upward to change the basic round shape into a four-lobed vase. Inside fingers steady and guide.

2. A more complex form is created by adding a small cylinder into the neck of a four-lobed vase form. The two clay pieces are joined together inside by pinching the clay to make a good weld.

3. The smaller cylinder is indented with the index finger to form four more lobes at the top. Extra clay is added to close the lobes and create four necks or spouts.

4. Five-lobed vase form was inspired by seed pods and made in the same manner as described above. G-Matt-3 Brown Glaze was applied thinly and reduction fired to Cone 10.

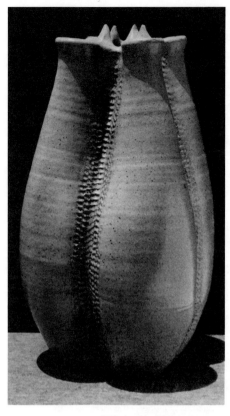

Far left: Vase fluted by indenting with the fingers to form four lobes. Sides are connected at top with extra clay to create four necks. Texture-wheel decoration in indentations. G-Matt-3 Gray-Green Glaze, Cone 10 reduction.

Left: Two-spouted flower container is functional and novel. The two lobes are cut apart and bent down; the space between is filled with a thrown sphere decorated with many smaller spouts. G-Matt-3 Glaze, Green-Brown. Cone 10 reduction.

The freshly-thrown cylinder is pushed in at the base with the index finger, then the finger is drawn up the wall with a light touch. This is repeated several times, starting with a strong pressure at the bottom and relaxing it slightly as the finger nears the top of the pot. As the outside finger travels upward, two fingers can be used opposite it on the inside to exert a gentle counter-pressure. This gives the potter better control and steadies the wall at the same time.

A similar indentation can be made on the opposite side of the pot to create another lobe. If two more indentations are made midway between the first ones, a four-lobed vase form results. If the pressure is increased at the top so that the four indentations nearly meet, balls of soft clay can be added here to connect the indentations and create four separate necks.

When the clay is firm, the base is trimmed by hand. Interest can be added by rolling a small texture wheel over the clay in the indentations.

A more complex shape can be made by deforming a tall cylinder into four lobes that do not quite close at the top. A smaller cylinder is thrown, cut from the wheel, placed into the opening of the lobed cylinder, and carefully pinched into place. This second cylinder is indented to form four lobes of its own that are joined at the top with extra clay to form spouts. The added clay is pinched into small points which give a nice emphasis to the top of this form. Of course, with a very large basic cylinder, it would be possible to add one or two more short cylinders to pyramid the form even more!

A variation of the lobed pot is made by starting with a tall cylindrical shape and indenting just the upper part so as to form two lobes that are pinched together at the top. The pinched area is cut downward from the top to form two separate spouts, and these are bent out from the center to create a shape somewhat similar to a tree trunk that divides into two smaller trunks. The area between the two spouts is filled in by throwing a closed sphere and incorporating it into the altered form. When this added clay has stiffened somewhat, small pellets of clay can be added to the sphere and pierced with a pencil to create many small spouts. This makes a novel, yet very functional container for flower arrangements.

Numberless variations can be made of any one decorating technique. Whenever the potter has the time, he should attempt to repeat an idea many times and introduce some variation into each in order to exploit the potentials.

Stamped Patterns and Textures

LIGHTWEIGHT INSULATING BRICK is a useful material in the pottery studio. It can be cut to make special sizes of shelf supports for inside the kiln, and it makes excellent stilts for supporting glazed ware. In addition to these uses, it is a wonderful material for making decorative patterns and textures in clay.

Insulating brick is made by adding ground-up walnut shells or cork to fireclay. When the brick is fired, the vegetable matter burns away, leaving a porous material that has excellent insulating properties and is light in weight.

Soft insulating brick can be purchased from brick and refractory sources, and is available for use at many different temperatures. The price per brick averages about fifty cents, but scraps sometimes can be obtained free from firms that manufacture or repair kilns, furnaces and incinerators. For decorating purposes, discarded brick is just as useful to the art potter as new brick. Broken ends can be used to produce beautiful textures. The soft brick can be cut with a saw, knife or even a stick of wood. Because it is a fragile material, however, it must be handled very gently.

Insulating brick is prepared for use as a decorating material by cutting it into a variety of sizes with the saw, then cutting or carving into the surfaces to make stamping or texturing blocks. Tools that can be used for carving include a hack saw, wood rasp, rattail file, triangular file, a nail, a dull paring knife, and almost anything else that will cut into the soft brick. The rasp or file can be used to round corners or ends; the hack saw can be used to cut patterns; and nails can be used to incise the brick surface. As you work, press the brick into some soft scrap clay to see the results. After you have made a number of different stamps, they can be tested on some pots.

I would recommend throwing several pots (or hand building them) for experimental decorating purposes. Set aside all but one of these pots; it can be left on the wheel for an experiment with wet clay. Press one of the insulating brick stamps into the soft clay wall and, at the same time, support the clay wall on the inside with your other hand. A gentle counter pressure will prevent the collapse or distortion of the wet clay form. Try rolling the stamp onto the clay, then rolling it off. Repeat one of the stamp designs in several patterns, or scramble a group of different stamp patterns in a random or accidental manner.

When working on very wet clay, you can expect the shape to become distorted; this is part of the freedom that comes with experimentation. Some of these trial pieces may turn out to be quite spontaneous and distinctive.

The pots that were set aside to stiffen should be just dry enough to hold their shapes well. A pot that is fairly leather hard may be too dry or stiff to impress with the stamps. Again, support the clay wall from the inside and actually press the clay out while the stamp is pressed into the outside surface to decorate it. Stronger impressions, those that are pressed deeply into the clay, produce the best results. Try repeating one stamp again and again on a shape for an all-over pattern. On another of the pots, try random placement of several different stamps. Remember that these are practice pots; don't be afraid to experiment on them.

1. An old paring knife is used to carve designs in pieces of porous insulating brick. As each stamp is made, it is tested on a scrap of soft clay.

2. An insulating brick stamp is pressed into the soft clay of a jar on the wheel while the wall is supported and pushed from within by the other hand.

3. The completed decoration is a textured repeat design that completely fills the space between foot and heavy lip. After bisque firing, slip is brushed into the indented areas.

4. Finished jar is glazed on the lip and inside with gray turquoise matt with ilmenite specks. Unglazed clay surface is orange with dark brown in the textured indented areas.

5. *Insulation brick was carved with an irregular pattern and pressed into the wet clay of this stoneware pot to give a random decoration.*

6. *The same stamp was used on a different wheel-thrown form for a totally different effect. A dark glaze was used at the rim of this pot.*

There are many techniques that might be used to complete these stamped pots. One of the most satisfactory is the use of a dark stain or slip after the pieces have been bisque fired. Try staining the whole surface with a thin coating of Barnard clay slip. This should be a mixture that is almost like muddy water; if it is too thick, the finished piece might resemble cast iron. Be certain that the pot is covered completely, with every single depression colored with the thin slip. Next, use a damp sponge to wipe the slip from the surface, leaving the slip only in the indented areas made by the stamps. It is necessary to sponge over and over, using clean water on the sponge, in order to get a satisfactory surface. For best results, the depressions should be dark, the high areas clean, and the medium-high areas just tinted with the slip.

The pots can be glazed either with strong colors or with colors that contrast to the dark slip. Colors that are similar to the dark brown of the slip will give no contrast and the decorating effort will be lost.

If you do not want to apply a glaze over the decorated area of the pot, you may glaze only the inside and perhaps the lip of the piece. If so, you may select a strong color or a contrasting glaze, such as black, white or turquoise. Brown probably wouldn't offer much contrast and it is doubtful whether it would do much for the piece.

If the outside surface is to be glazed, a thin coating of a transparent or translucent matt glaze can be effective over the stain. The depressions would be dark brown and the high areas would be clear or semi-clear. Because most transparent glazes are glossy, these are best when used on small pots. Other glazes I could recommend are a thin coating of White Glaze, Oatmeal Glaze, or Pale Blue Waxy Matt Glaze. Colored clear glazes might be good, and the Celadon, Dark Celadon, and Transparent Blue Chun Glaze would be excellent.

Paddling

MANY EXCITING CHANGES can be made on the form and surface of a clay shape simply by beating it with the edge or side of a square stick. A wooden paddle may be notched with a knife, studded with upholstery tacks, or wrapped with cord and used by the adventurous and creative craftsman to produce unusual shapes and surface treatment on soft clay pots.

A large firebrick stamp, a piece of split or broken wood, or the heavily textured bark on a stick of firewood can also be used effectively to paddle and reshape a pot while it is being textured. No matter how the piece is formed or what tools are used for paddling, a strong, rugged, and very individual statement in clay will be the result. The process of beating clay in this manner is excellent for adding texture and character to hand-built forms as well as to wheel-thrown shapes.

The basic shape of a pot influences the way in which it can be altered successfully by paddling. A paddled effect that looks good on a simple bottle shape may not be at all attractive on a double gourd form. The form as thrown on the wheel may even need to be squeezed and reshaped in the hands before the surface is paddled for texture and refinement of form.

The condition of the clay is extremely important for success with the paddling technique. The clay shape should be stiff enough to handle but still be soft enough to be deformed by firm pressure. When the clay is at the proper consistency for paddling, it is very tough and it will withstand an amazing amount of paddling.

If the clay is too stiff, the paddling action will crack the wall. If the top edge becomes too dry, as it very well may, this area may crack when the form is altered. To prevent this, the rim can be immersed in water as often as is needed in order to keep its consistency the same as the rest of the pot.

Paddling the clay is a good way to change a round wheel-thrown shape into a squared one. The lower portion of a tall bottle might be flattened and textured with a large piece of insulating firebrick or a broken stick to produce a squared bottle with a round shoulder and neck. Other materials that might be used to alter the shape and provide similar surface textures include a stout roll of corrugated cardboard, a squashed tin can, or a wooden dowel rod.

The potter has many choices for finishing a piece that has been altered and textured by the paddling technique. The bisque-fired pot might simply be glazed to produce a very handsome result. Thin Barnard clay slip might be sponged on the surface, then wiped off the high areas with a clean, dampened sponge. A similar effect can be obtained by using a thin slip of red iron oxide instead of the Barnard clay slip. If the glaze firing is to be in an oxidation atmosphere, a thin mixture of manganese dioxide and water could be used to stain the depressions in the surface of the bisque-fired pot.

A light-colored translucent matt glaze can be used effectively over the stain because the colorant will bleed through the glaze just enough to provide a rich and unusual effect. The potter may decide to glaze just the inside of the pot and leave the textured outside surface decorated with the slip alone.

1. *A basic shape may be altered while it is textured. Here, the bottom section of a tall bottle is paddled with a large piece of carved insulating firebrick.*

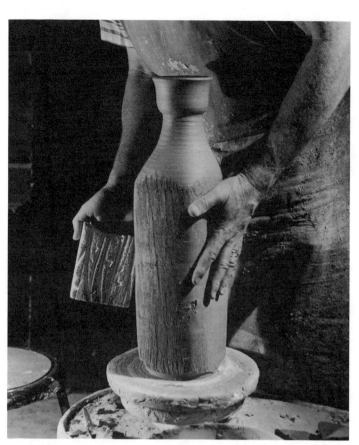

2. *Paddling has squared the bottle and given a fine texture to the surface. The reverse side of the pot is supported while the shape is being altered.*

3. *A broken section of stick is used to paddle the same pot. This texture is more pronounced and gives a better decorative effect than the first attempt.*

4. *Finished bottle was glazed with a very thin coating of White G-Matt-3 Glaze. A light glaze application was used so that the textural effect would remain dominant.*

14

5. The base of a freshly-thrown pot is squeezed between the hands to give it a new shape before final forming and texturing are done with the paddle.

6. When the clay has stiffened enough so that it can be handled, the edge of a square stick is repeatedly hammered into two sides to create a vertical pattern.

7. The end of the stick is used to paddle a completely different vertical texture pattern into the unbeaten end sections of the reshaped vase form.

8. After bisque firing, the indented areas of the oval vase were stained with a dilute Barnard clay slip, then covered with Waxy White Glaze before the final firing.

Top left: Coarse texture on this hand-built stoneware pot was paddled-on with a piece of firewood that still retained its heavy bark. Top was glazed with Waxy Black Matt.

Top right: Cylindrical vase was flattened, then paddled with edge of a square stick. Clay bridges were added at top to form three openings, then paddled lightly for added texture.

Left: Double gourd-shaped bottle was altered into a modified fluting effect by paddling with the corner of a square stick. White G-Matt-3 Glaze used over dark slip in the depressions.

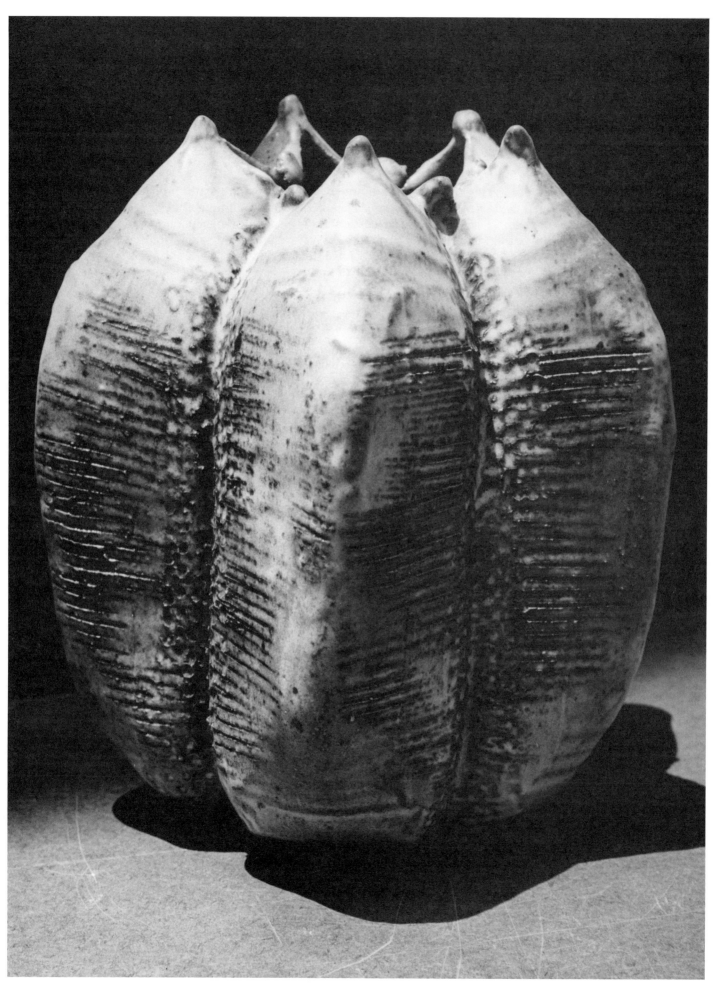

Rolling a Pattern

THE TECHNIQUE OF ROLLING A PATTERN into clay is as old as pottery itself. The Babylonians, Assyrians, and Persians used this idea with their cuneiform writing. Chinese, European and pre-Columbian South American Indian potters used rolled patterns on their pots. This is a good example of the value of studying the art and techniques of past cultures—not for copying, but for a new application of an old idea.

The idea of decorating pots in this manner started for me with a visit to a cactus garden. The forms and textures of cacti were so beautiful and intriguing that it seemed a good idea to try to reflect them in clay. This idea led to a roller tool for reproducing patterns suggestive of the texture of trunks of trees. In turn, trunks of various trees suggested new patterns and textures that required new tools to obtain varied forms and surface treatments of pottery. This sharpens one's observation and appreciation of nature. The whole experience can be exciting and very challenging.

To the imaginative and creative craftsman, the variations of tools and textures are as endless as the variations in the trunks of trees in a forest. For that reason, every piece of pottery made will be distinctive and individual.

The easiest, most creative tools are those you shape for yourself. Casters made for furniture are fine; old fashioned wooden-wheel casters are best but the new hard-rubber or plastic casters are also good. An electric grinding wheel can be used to carve patterns in the casters, and this works easily and quickly. A saw or file works well also. For a ready-made wheel, try the notched wheel used to put an edge on piecrust, or a meat-tenderizer tool. A wheel could be made by putting a bronze gear on a handle. A springerle cookie roller is another ready-made decorating tool.

The most flexible material of all for a texture wheel is clay. You can carve a solid cylinder of clay by hand or make it on the wheel and allow it to become leather hard. Next, the center hole can be drilled in the cylinder and the thickness you wish can be sliced off. The design is carved in the clay deeply and with sharp edges. When dry, the wheel should be fired to mature the clay so that the tool will be very hard. A wooden or heavy-wire handle can be made for the wheel, a small stove bolt can be used for the axle, a number of washers can be used for spacers, and two or more nuts can be added so that one nut will act as a back or stop for the other.

The texture tool works best when the pot is in the soft-leather-hard condition. The thrown piece may be left on the wheel for decoration, firmly attached to the throwing head or a throwing bat. The wheel is turned at a fairly slow speed as the texture tool is applied on the outside with one hand. The other hand supports the inside wall of the pot as it turns slowly on the wheel. The tool is pressed firmly on the clay so that it will make a pattern from the bottom to the top without stopping.

A sharp metal texture tool will work on a pot that is stiffer than leather hard. Some texture wheels will work on very wet clay pots if the walls of the pot are quite thick.

After bisque firing, the pots are glazed inside. The outside can be glazed with a transparent colored glaze; matt glazes and opaque glazes are not too effective. A textured bisque surface can simply be left unglazed. Try sponging Barnard clay slip thinly onto the bisque texture, then wipe the surface of the texture clean with a sponge. Next dip the neck or rim of the pot in glaze just to the edge of the texture and glaze fire the pot—it will work nicely.

It is possible to treat the texture in another way to give an intriguing finish. Glaze the inside of the bisque pot. Dip a sponge in a darkly colored glaze and sponge the glaze deeply into the texture. Wet your hands and rub them over the texture to push the dark glaze into the texture. Try to fill the depressions and wipe the high points clean of glaze. Now cover the entire pot with a white or light-colored glaze, and fire. The dark glaze should bleed through the light glaze and give a beautiful finish.

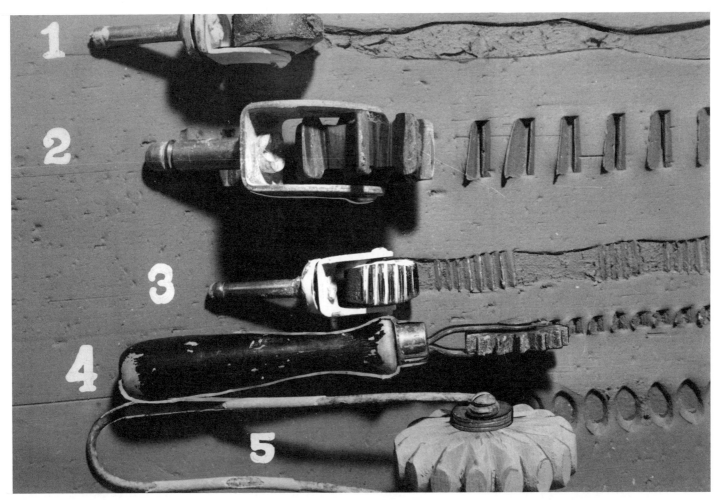

1. Home-made tools make it possible to reproduce some of the texture inspired by nature. Each tool has left its mark, just as an auto leaves its tire marks on a muddy road. 1 is a hard-rubber caster from a chest; the sides were ground down to make a wavy-broad line. 2 is a large synthetic plastic caster shaped by cutting sections on a band saw. 3 is a wooden caster ground to shape on a sanding disc, then notched with a three-corner metal file. 4 is a fence-stretching tool; the wheel resembles the Spanish spur worn by western cowboys. 5 is a slice of an old wooden rolling pin with pattern filed in with a wood rasp. The handle is a piece of wire from a coat hanger.

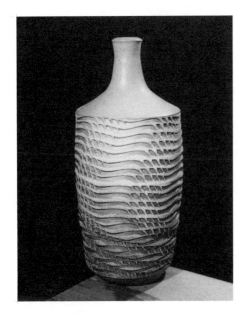

Stoneware bottle textured with a carved plastic furniture caster. Textured area was stained with Barnard clay slip; glaze used was Waxy Blue-Green.

Wide mouth of this jar allowed the potter to support the wall from within and apply the rolled texture while the clay was still quite moist.

Rolled-on pattern came from a cut furniture caster. Top was dipped in Waxy Blue-Green Glaze, then in Waxy White Glaze to achieve the bubbled effect.

Convex Fluting

POTTERS HAVE ALWAYS BEEN an inventive group of craftsmen. Most potters I have known have invented tools and equipment for their own use or have adapted them from tools and equipment originally made for some other purpose.

One of the simplest and most effective tools I have ever made is a wooden one for making decorative convex fluting on pottery. Convex fluting may be described as curved sectioning that resembles the segments found on a pumpkin and some varieties of melon and squash. This type of fluting has been used for many centuries as a decoration on columns; it has been used just as long for ornamentation on pottery forms.

A tool for fluting can be made from a thin strip of hard maple, walnut, teak or any other close-grained hard wood. The strip should be about 1/8 inch thick, 2 inches wide and 4 or 5 inches long. The fluting tool is shaped by using an electric belt sander or even a grinding wheel to grind the wood into the shapes shown in the illustration. Naturally, the shaping can be done by other means, but this method is fast and effective for making curves. Because requirements vary on almost every piece you want to decorate by this means, you may wish to make several different fluting tools, each one different in size, angle and curve.

The pottery shapes that best lend themselves to fluting are the rather swelling, curved ones, although cylindrical forms also can be used to good effect. The pots themselves may be thrown on the wheel, may be slab or coil built, or perhaps might be thickly-cast greenware.

What is most important for the technique of fluting is the consistency of the clay. The clay form should be leather hard — firm but still slightly flexible. It should be firm enough to handle with care but too wet to trim.

In preparation for fluting, the shape's circumference must be divided into sections; a good number of sections for the beginner to attempt is eight. Mark the divisions on the clay near the top of the form and draw vertical lines toward the bottom. An easy method for making vertical lines is to fill a small syringe with some blue ink that is diluted with water. Hold the syringe at one of the division marks near the top of the pot and squeeze gently to release a large drop of ink onto the clay surface. This will run straight down the side and give an accurate line to follow for the fluting process.

The actual process of fluting is simple and can be done quickly and efficiently when you have had just a little practice. Fluting is done by gently incising the vertical lines with a fluting tool. It is important to note that the point of the tool should be slightly rounded or blunted; otherwise it will cut too deeply into the clay and possibly go completely through the wall. A properly blunted working point only scrapes a very small amount of clay from the pot. The main action of the fluting tool is to model the clay and gently push it inward. It is important to start with a slight pressure and work on each vertical line in turn. Repeat the process, each time pushing a little harder until the lines are deeply enough incised to create the effect of convex fluting in the areas between the lines.

Because of the resulting irregularity in the surface caused by fluting, it is difficult to footrim a wheel-thrown pot in the usual manner. In most cases it is best to trim the bottom by hand when the pot is firm enough to hold and work on.

Inspiration for fluted shapes can be found in nature in the form of some of the seed pods, fruit, nuts and in the squash, melon and pumpkin family. In addition to inspiration for the fluted shapes themselves, these natural forms are excellent to refer to for ideas on texturing and glazing.

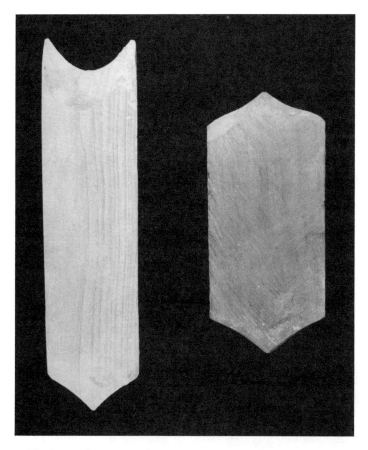

1. Fluting tools were made from thin slabs of hard maple wood shaped on an electric grinding wheel. The tools vary in size, angle and curve.

2. Convex fluting tool is used to carve and model the segments of a fluted vase. Consistency of clay should be firm but still flexible for best results.

Fluted vase is an example of a shape inspired by a form found in nature.

Fluted vase was made from stoneware clay and glazed to enhance its decorative form.

21

Concave Fluting

WHEN BERNARD LEACH first made a tour of the United States, he conducted a workshop at Mills College. During that visit, we came across some pictures of ancient fluted pottery and I asked Mr. Leach how the fluting was done. He replied that he had learned how to make and use fluting tools when he studied pottery in Japan, that it was quite simple and that we would make a fluting tool the next day. Since I had laboriously tried fluting a pot using a wire loop modeling tool and found it to be inadequate, I looked forward to seeing what Mr. Leach would do.

The next morning we went to the metal shop in search of some metal from which to make a fluting tool. After looking at the sheets of copper and brass that I had on hand, Mr. Leach observed that he would prefer a piece of iron barrel hoop, for that was what he usually used. We finally found what he wanted in the college maintenance shop when we stumbled upon an old wooden barrel that was still held together with a number of rusty but adequate iron hoops.

To make the fluting tool, we cut some of this metal into a piece that was one inch wide and six inches in length, then hammered it flat. Approximately an inch from one end, we drilled a half-inch hole through the iron strip. To make this hole *concave*, the metal strip was placed on a wooden stump and the rounded end of a ball peen hammer was positioned on the hole. By striking the upturned flat end of the peen hammer with the flat surface of a claw hammer, the hole was given the concave shape that Bernard Leach wanted. Since the iron was a soft metal, this operation was quite easy.

The next step was to fasten the iron strip loosely in a vise so that about two-thirds of the hole was confined. The strip was bent at this point into a 45-degree angle, and the tool was finished and ready for use.

Bernard Leach then selected a leather-hard porcelain bowl that he had made the day before, turned it upside down on a table so that nearly a quarter of the bowl extended over the table edge. Then in about three minutes of seemingly-casual work, the potter fluted the bowl with exquisite sharp-edged diagonal fluting. It was truly amazing to see how beautifully the tool worked and how simple the whole process appeared!

22

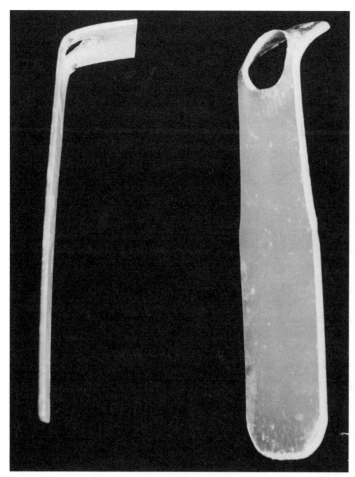

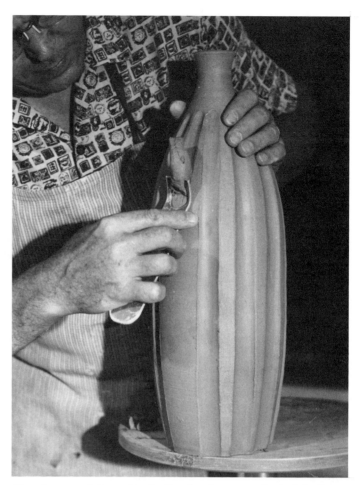

Fluting tools are made from fairly thick pieces of aluminum. A hole is drilled at one end and hammered into a concave shape, then the metal is bent to a 45-degree angle.

Clay is gouged from the leather-hard pot as the tool is drawn downward from the neck. The stroke is repeated around the shape to achieve the fluted effect.

Recently I wanted to do some fluting and therefore looked for the fluting tool that Mr. Leach had made. However, I couldn't find it and knew that I would have to make a fluting tool. In the metal shop I located a fairly thick piece of aluminum and, deciding to try this metal instead of iron, I used the Leach technique to make the tools illustrated in the photograph. The aluminum worked quite well and the tools are good ones, although the cutting edges may not last as long as those of iron tools. However, they can be sharpened with a round file. I should think that the same tool could be made from brass or bronze.

For your first experiments in using a concave fluting tool, I suggest that you work on cylindrical forms that have walls slightly thicker than you usually use. Perhaps fluting would be a good technique to use on pots that are too heavy. The fluting takes away enough clay to make them at least a little bit lighter.

The pot should be in the leather-hard condition—too wet to trim but stiff enough to handle. Start at the top of the cylinder and, using a firm stroke, take a good gouge of clay out of the wall as you move the tool downward. When the cut is complete, repeat the stroke around the shape to achieve the fluted effect. It usually is not necessary to measure for the spacing of fluted areas; as you make the final three or four scoops, you can adjust the spacing by eye to finish fluting the form evenly.

This technique is simple and effective. With just a small amount of practice, anyone should be able to make some very handsome pots with concave fluted surfaces.

Trailed Slip Transfer

TRAILING A SLIP DECORATION on the vertical surface of a pot can be a very frustrating experience. The first application of slip for the design usually goes on quite easily and looks good. However, when the pot is nearly half covered with a satisfactory raised line decoration, difficulties appear. The decorator wants to hold the pot horizontally or at an angle so that the slip won't run in the wrong direction, but can't tip or tilt the piece because there is no area for holding it that will not mean the ruin of at least a portion of the design. Even if the first application of slip is allowed to dry before continuing, there still is a great risk of marring the design by handling the pot. The simple and effective method presented here for applying a raised line decoration makes use of the principle of transferring a decoration from one surface to another. This method of decorating a leather-hard pot is fast, direct and effective. In addition, it is fascinating and fun to do.

The slip must be one that "fits" the clay body being used. The slip may be made from the same clay you are using or it may be made from another clay which fits the clay body perfectly. You may wish to use the slip in its natural color or you may decide to color it with stains, underglazes or oxides.

The clay slip can be prepared from trimming scraps or lumps of any dry clay. The first step is to crush the dry scrap clay and sprinkle this into a pan that contains some water. Let this stand about 20 minutes while the clay disintegrates or slakes in the water. Next, stir the slip mixture until no lumps remain. It may be necessary to screen the mixture or beat it with a mixer if lumps remain. Some fine grog may be added if desired. More water or more clay can be added to get the desired consistency of a thick paste that is still fluid but will not run off your hand.

The slip trailer I use is a large plastic bag in which a frozen chicken or turkey is packaged, but any plastic can be used if it is fairly heavy and sturdy. The slip is placed in the bag and then the bag is bounced on the table surface to force air bubbles from the slip. The next step is to squeeze the air out of the bag and close the bag by tying it securely with a piece of string. The bag of slip is ready for use and will stay in workable condition for many months.

The pot should be leather hard for this method of slip decoration and it is a good idea to sponge some water on the surface just before the application of the slip. I would like to add a word of caution here: I applied slip by this technique to a freshly thrown pot and then set it aside in the damp box to stiffen. The next day I discovered that the pot had collapsed into a pile of wet clay. The water from the slip evidently had weakened the pot and caused its downfall!

Slip decoration is started by using a piece of newspaper or paper towel on which to slip trail. The slip trailer itself is made by cutting a corner from the slip-filled plastic bag. The hole should be small. By squeezing the plastic bag, a raised slip pattern is trailed onto the surface of the paper. This pattern of slip is transferred to the pot by lifting the piece of paper and pressing the slip against the surface of the pot. The slip can be pressed on the pot gently to produce one effect, or it may be pressed harder for a flatter squashed-line effect. The paper is peeled from the pot and the raised slip design is in place! This process can be repeated until the whole pot is decorated to your satisfaction.

When a successful decoration has been done, the piece is dried slowly and carefully and then it is bisque fired before any further decorating is done. One good method for finishing a piece done by this decorative technique is to first glaze the inside of the pot, then sponge or spray on the outside a very thin slip made from Barnard clay and water. As soon as the surface is covered, most of the slip is sponged off the surface with a damp sponge. This leaves a dark brown color in the depressions, a thin orange-brown film on some areas, and the color of the clay body on the high areas. The final step is to dip the neck or top portion of the pot in the same glaze used on the inside. When the glaze is dry, the piece is fired and a very pleasant effect results.

Thick clay slip is squeezed from an improvised plastic bag trailer to form a pattern on a piece of newspaper.

The paper is lifted in the hands and the slip pattern is pressed against the side of a leather-hard pot.

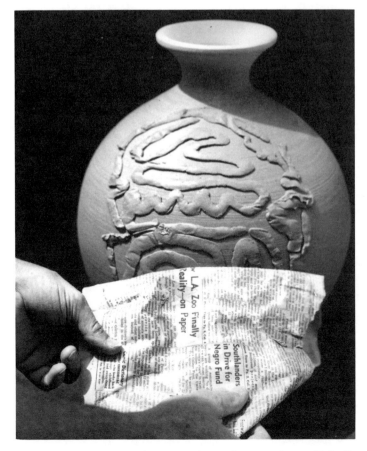

When the paper is peeled away from the pot, the trailed slip decoration has been transferred to the surface.

Similar trailed slip patterns are transferred to the surface to continue the decoration around the pot.

Trailed Slip Texture

Shell of sea urchin washed up onto the beach shows one example of the textures found in nature.

A WONDERFUL SOURCE OF INSPIRATION for pottery is in the multitude of little things in nature that we look at without really seeing. For example, the sea urchin tossed up onto the beach is fun to find, admire and then toss aside. The bark on a tree might be quite beautiful, yet be ignored simply because there is bark on all of the trees that line the streets where we walk. The seed pod—so beautiful in detail, so wonderful to touch and so inspiring as a suggested form for a pottery container—falls from the tree and is crushed under our feet.

It is distressing that so many of these beautiful works of Mother Nature go unseen and unappreciated! However, these wonders will not be wasted if we, as potters, translate just a small portion of them into the more permanent and enduring form of fired clay.

In my observation of sea urchins, tree bark and seed pods in the West Coast area where I live and work, I found examples of each that had one characteristic in common: all had textural effects consisting of cone-shaped protuberances. Now, this is a decorative effect that has a great appeal to me as a potter. Such an effect can be suggested by fashioning small conical shapes by hand and attaching them to a pot, of course, but this is a laborious and boring process. A much simpler method for making and attaching these swelling appendages consists of the use of slip and the improvised slip trailer mentioned in the preceding project.

A thick slip is made by collecting clay trimming scraps and crushing them when they are dry. This dry scrap is covered with water, allowed to soak for about ten minutes, then it is stirred thoroughly and the consistency adjusted either by adding more clay or more water to bring the slip to about the consistency of mayonnaise. When this stage is reached, the slip is screened to remove any lumps.

The slip trailer is easily made by selecting a plastic bag and filling its lower portion with the slip. The bag is closed and tied just above the mass of slip, then a trailing spout is made by snipping a corner off the bottom of the bag with a pair of scissors. Pressure on the bag forces slip from the improvised slip trailer and the potter can check the results to see whether the consistency of slip or the size of the trailing hole need to be changed. Naturally, some practice, experiments and adjustments must take place before you can become an expert slip trailer.

The exact effect you are striving to achieve for your decoration will determine the precise method of application of slip to the greenware pot. The accompanying photographs tell most of the story; however, there are some precautions that should be noted.

The thick slip should not be applied to a freshly-thrown pot because there is a chance that the water in the slip, added to the wet pot, may cause the shape to collapse. I recommend that the pot be allowed to stiffen or dry a short time until the clay becomes *firm* but still is wet.

The slip should be made from the same clay used for making the pot. This insures a correct fit of slip to the clay shape. This slip may be colored in order to give a particular effect but great care should be taken to avoid a garish, overdone decoration.

This technique is so easy to do, and it is such fun, that the main caution really is to avoid going too far with it. Remember that you are decorating a pot, not a birthday cake.

1. Seed pod from a flowering tree provided the inspiration for a pot with slip-trailed texture.

2. Detail of the bark of a tree is another example of knobby protuberances found in nature.

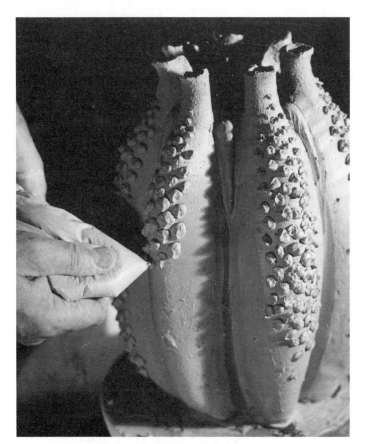

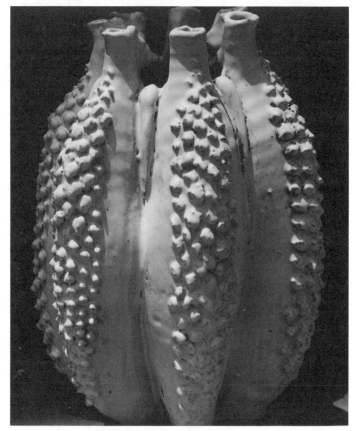

3. Cones of thick slip are extruded from a plastic bag trailer onto a leather-hard multiform vase.

4. After bisque firing, the vase was coated with a thick waxy glaze and fired again.

Feather Combing

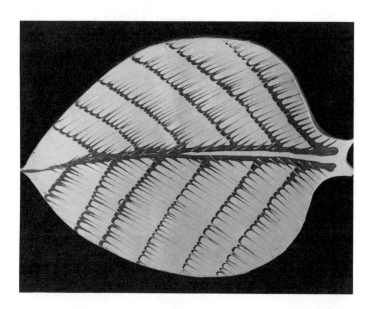

FOR MANY YEARS I HAD ADMIRED THE INTRICATE COMBED SLIP designs that resemble cake decorations. I could find no books that explained the process, however, and assumed that "combed slip" was done by pulling a pocket comb through a layer of wet slip. When I tried this, the effect was just what might be expected and not even close to the marvelous patterns achieved by European potters. Then one day Bernard Leach spent a morning demonstrating trailed and combed slip to a group of California potters and the secrets of the technique were revealed.

The secrets of the technique are simple but subtle. The clay form to be decorated must be wet but not too wet. A heavy layer of thick slip is applied all over the surface and into this is trailed a pattern of thick slip of a contrasting color. The tip of a feather, a fine splinter of bamboo or a piece of fine metal wire is pulled through the slip and this drags one slip color into the other in a delicate thread of a line. This is the wonderfully exciting part of the technique that Mr. Leach referred to as "feather combing."

While feather combing can be done on a wheel-thrown shape, it is best done on a slab of rolled-out clay. When the decoration has "set up" a bit, the slab is shaped over a hump mold.

A clay slab is rolled out to the desired size and thickness, then placed on a board so that it can be handled easily. A quantity of thick slip is poured onto the slab, then the board and slab are tilted in various directions to completely cover the clay surface with a thick layer of slip. Finally, the board is thumped sharply onto the table to level the surface of the slip.

A contrasting color of slip is selected for trailing. For example, if dark brown slip is used to cover the slab, a white slip might be used for the trailing. Trailing can be done with a rubber syringe filled with slip. Straight lines of the white slip are extruded from the syringe across the base coat of brown slip. For a first attempt at this process, I would suggest making the lines about ½ inch apart. You will notice that the trailed slip sinks down slightly into the base coat of slip. It must be emphasized that both slips must be thick but wet. If the background slip is thin or dry when the contrasting slip is trailed over it, the technique won't work.

Combing is done with the tip of a stiff feather. This may be a chicken feather or one from a pigeon, gull or whatever you are able to find. The feather is drawn very lightly across the surface of the slip at right angles to the trailed lines. Because the slip is still wet, the two

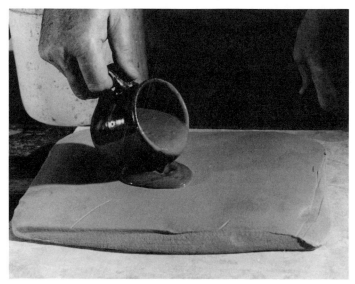

1. A slab of clay is rolled out on a board, then a large quantity of very thick colored slip is poured out on the surface of the slab.

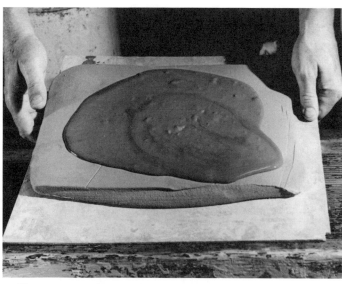

2. The board is lifted and tilted in different directions in order to almost completely cover the slab with an even layer of the thick slip.

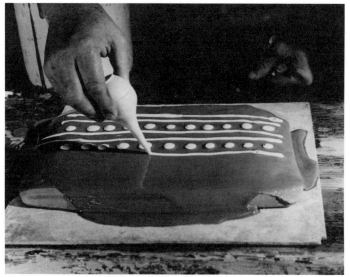

3. A syringe is filled with a contrasting color of slip. This slip is extruded onto the dark slip to form a pattern of lines and dots.

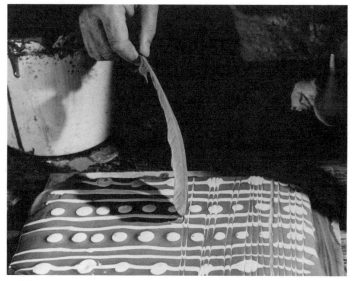

4. The tip of a feather is pulled across the surface to drag one color of slip into another and thus create an unusual decorative pattern.

colors are pulled into one another. The feather-combed lines are repeated, either at regular or uneven intervals, close together or far apart, and all in one direction or in a reverse pattern. All of these variations make interesting space arrangements.

The feather used for trailing is easier to handle if the quill is nearly stripped, leaving feathers on the tip alone. Other tools that may be used for combing include a splinter of bamboo, a piece of very thin wire, or even a piece of heavy nylon fishline. A needle is too stiff.

You may want to try combinations of other slip colors for some variation in this work. The trailed lines needn't be straight, but might be wavy or circular. Large blobs of slip may be used instead of trailed lines, or in addition to them.

A marbled effect can be obtained with the combed design by lifting the slab on its board, tilting it slightly, then giving it a sharp little shake or two. This is a good technique to try with designs that have not been very successful. Because the feather-combing method is so very much fun to do, it is more than likely that the first few attempts will result in over-decorated pieces.

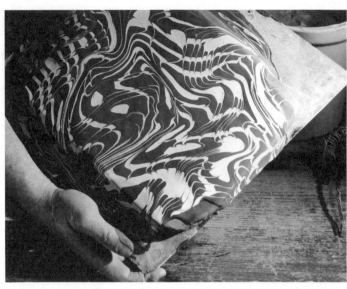

5. A heavy piece of nylon fishline can be used to comb the slip. A broom straw, a fine metal wire or a splinter of bamboo also could be used.

6. A marbled slip pattern can be made by lifting the board and shaking it sharply in one or two different directions to make the slip move slightly.

Feather combing can be done on wheel-thrown shapes but it is a tricky process. First attempts should be made on shallow forms such as plates or low bowls with wide foot areas and rather thick walls. After they have been thrown, they should be set aside to stiffen a bit; they should be firm but not dry enough for trimming.

Several syringes are prepared with slip for trailing and a quantity of slip is made up for the background. The background slip is poured into the centered bowl that is revolving on the wheel and spread with the fingers or a brush to cover the surface with a layer of the slip that is thick enough to retain its position on the sloping surface and not run down and pool in the center of the bowl. The syringes are used to add the lines or blobs of contrasting-colored slip over the background slip. When this is done, the feather is used to comb the design.

It takes a number of failures to learn to decorate with this technique, and I would like to mention a few precautions that must be taken. If the thrown clay form is too wet, the wet slip may cause the bowl to collapse. If the clay shape is too dry, the background slip may set too quickly and dry out too much for successful combing. It is not easy to find the ideal conditions for clay shapes and thickness of the slips, but it can be done through experimentation and much patient work.

Cylindrical forms can be decorated with feather combing, but the results are more limited than on flat or shallow shapes. The centered cylinder is rotated on the wheel and the outside is coated with the background slip. The contrasting slip is applied with a syringe but the manner of application is much different than that used for the bowl. The wheel is stopped and the syringe is held in one place near the top and slip extruded; instead of staying in one place, the slip runs down the side in a straight vertical line. This is repeated by moving the syringe about 1/2 inch and extruding again to make another vertical line. When the pot is covered with spaced vertical lines, the wheel is rotated and a feather is used to comb a design in horizontal or spiraling bands. This same technique can be used with two or more colored slips for the trailing process.

Bisque-fired pots decorated with feather combing are generally glazed with colorless transparents because the color already exists in the slips. If additional color is wanted for the glaze, a delicate tint, such as the Celadon, is best. If the slip colors are too strong, a thin layer of translucent glaze may be needed to subdue the effect. White Waxy Glaze works very well for this purpose.

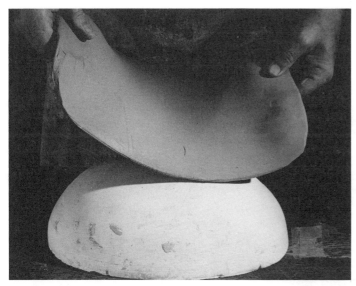

7. When the slip has stiffened to the leather-hard stage, the slab can be lifted, inverted and placed over a hump mold to give it a new shape.

8. The outside surface of the slab may be textured at the same time that it is shaped to the mold. Here a piece of coarse porous firebrick is used for texture.

9. A potter's knife is used to cut through the clay and form the desired shape for the pot. Excess clay is peeled from the slab as it is cut.

10. Small wads of clay can be added to the bottom and incorporated into the slab in order to form legs or feet of the desired height.

A Combed Slip Variation

*Far left: Stoneware lamp base dec-
orated with finger-combed clay slip.
Brown G-Matt-3 Glaze.*

*Left: Stoneware vase trailed with
slip and combed with a finger.
Green-Brown G-Matt-3 Glaze; Cone
10 reduction.*

THE SLIP COMBING DECORATION TECHNIQUE provides a point of departure for another decoration method that is rich in possibilities. This technique uses thick clay slip to create a raised decoration on a green pot.

The first step is to throw a vase shape and let it stiffen or dry a short while until the clay becomes firm but still is quite wet. While the pot is drying to this condition, prepare the slip.

Scrap clay or clay trimmings can be used to make the slip. Use the same clay as was used for making the pot. It should be crushed, covered with water and allowed to soak for about ten minutes so that the clay can "slake." It should then be stirred thoroughly and its consistency adjusted if necessary. This can be done by adding either more clay or more water until the clay assumes the consistency of mayonnaise. The last step in the preparation of the slip is to force it through a 30-mesh screen to remove any lumps.

The slip trailer I use is a plastic bag. Select a rather large one and roll down the edges so that it is easier to fill the lower portion of the bag with slip. When the slip has been added to the plastic bag, bounce the bag on the table top a few times to force any air bubbles to the surface for removal. Then tie the bag closed just above the mass of slip.

Next, take a pair of scissors and snip off one corner of the plastic bag. Make just a small cut and then squeeze some clay from the bag to see the size of line that is extruded. If you desire a larger line, cut the hole larger. Now the slip trailer is ready.

When the pot is stiff enough to continue work, center it exactly on the wheel and fasten it to the wheel head. *It must be centered perfectly.* Decorating is done by holding the bag of slip in the hands and extruding clay from it as the pot revolves at slow or medium speed. Start at the top and try to trail a band of slip on the pot in a slow downward motion; don't stop until you reach the bottom. This will produce a spiral effect. If this first effort is a failure, scrape the applied slip from the surface of the pot with a rib and try again. It may take several attempts before you develop the skill needed to trail the slip successfully.

1. Heavy clay slip is trailed from a plastic bag as the centered pot revolves on the wheel at a slow speed.

2. When the trailing is complete, a finger is dragged through the fresh slip vertically from bottom to top.

The decoration can be considered finished at this point or you may wish to do some "combing." This can be done by pulling a finger up vertically through the slip from the bottom to the top of the pot. This can be repeated several times at intervals around the circumference of the clay shape. Different effects can be achieved by substituting a modeling tool, feather or a brush for the finger.

There is another approach to decoration that can be used and this might appeal to you if you have a failure with the combing technique. The pot can be covered with a thick, irregular layer of slip, then a finger dragged through the slip to make a series of vertical grooves running from bottom to top. Next, the wheel is set in motion and a pointed tool is used to describe a spiral line through the soft clay slip from the top to the bottom of the pot.

There are, of course, many ways in which you can achieve variety in the use of this technique. Perhaps colored slip could be used. In this case I want to emphasize that the slip should be made from the same clay used for the body of the pot. By so doing there will be no chance that the slip will shrink, crack or fall off the piece of pottery.

Pieces of pottery decorated in this manner should turn out to be very beautiful whether they are glazed or not. In some instances the harmony of the shape and decoration might well be upset by the addition of glaze. And of course the proper glaze treatment might enhance one of these trailed and combed decorations.

I think I should caution against letting yourself become "carried away" with this technique and creating mere frosting. Above all, do not force the materials to do things that are not in harmony with clay forms. If the decoration fits the technique and the materials, the result should be good.

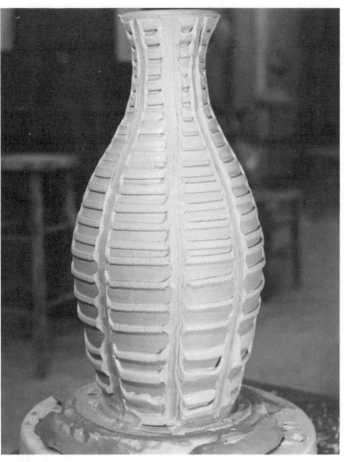 

3. The slip decoration is complete and the pot ready for firing as soon as it is dry.

4. Another example of slip-trailed and combed decoration on a wheel-thrown piece.

Close-up photo shows detail of combed slip texture on the piece pictured on page 32.

Slip Inlay

JAPANESE POTTERS ALWAYS HAVE BEEN INFLUENCED by Korean pottery and one of the Korean techniques greatly admired and emulated by the Japanese has been clay slip inlay. They call the technique "mishima," and the same term is sometimes used by American potters to describe this particular decorating method.

Briefly, the technique consists of incising some sort of pattern into the surface of a moist greenware pot, then filling these areas with layers of colored slip. When the pot is dry, the surface is scraped, leaving a sharp, distinct pattern of one color against a contrasting one. After bisque firing, the piece is covered with a thin-to-medium layer of transparent glaze and fired again. The Korean ware so greatly admired was made from a buff-colored clay, inlaid with black or white slip, and glazed with a pale celadon or colorless glaze that was reduction fired.

The best clay to use for inlay is a smooth, fine-textured one with no grog or sand added. If a coarse-grained clay is used, the incised decoration should be bold because the sand or grog will scratch the surface when it is scraped to remove the excess slip. Sometimes this gives an interesting texture, but it usually is at some sacrifice to the design.

There are many methods that can be used to incise a design, but most potters wish to do this in a simple, rapid manner. It would take many hours to carve these areas by hand, and this time might better be spent carving some stamps for pressing into the leather-hard clay pot. Stamps can be carved from firm pieces of moist clay, then bisque fired; they can be carved from plaster; they can be carved from soft insulating brick; or small ones can be made by filing designs into the heads of nails.

Stamping tools may be "found." Old or new buttons make excellent incising or stamping tools. A piece of iron wire can be threaded through the holes in a button and used as a handle for pressing. Leather-stamping tools are good for imprinting, as are pieces of rubber or metal type, costume jewelry, metal drawer or door pulls, and carved wooden ornaments.

A stamp can be made from one of these "found" objects by pressing soft clay into the design, pulling it away gently, then allowing the clay to dry before it is bisque fired. Because the clay will not harm the objects into which it is impressed, even valuable pieces of art may be utilized for the purpose of making stamps. When such stamps are placed in unusual juxtapositions on contemporary pieces, the activity can be quite creative and the results beautiful. Imagine an elaborate pot shape incised with some buttons, metal house numbers, leather-stamping tools, and a garland pattern from an ancient Roman ornament! It may sound crazy but it very well might be handsome.

A nearly-dry vase was incised with a section of saw blade, then inlaid with blue engobe. Glazed with White G-Matt-3 and reduction fired to Cone 10.

Nature also provides wonderful objects that can be utilized for stamping. A peach pit, black walnut shell, and seed pod make excellent patterns.

A favorite technique of some Japanese potters consists of pressing a short piece of rope on the inside of a bowl for a very distinctive pattern.

Incising can be done on the clay pots that have become too dry for stamping but still are slightly damp. A short section of a hacksaw blade, a steel rib with serrated edge, steel plaster tools, a grapefruit knife, or an apple corer can be used to carve designs and textures into the clay.

When the incising has been done, the surface of the pot is coated with an engobe or colored clay slip that provides some contrast to the body color. If the clay used for the slip is the same as that of the body, it can be colored as desired. The first layer of engobe applied should be rather thin; subsequent coatings may be thicker. Each layer should be allowed to dry for a while before the next is applied to give it ample time for drying shrinkage. It is important that the depressions be covered completely with slip.

When the pot is dry, the surface is scraped to remove the excess slip and leave sharp patterns where the slip filled the incised areas. Scraping must be done carefully to avoid going too deeply and perhaps eliminating parts of the design. The surface can be scraped with a knife or steel rib, or it can be sanded with a piece of Styrofoam. This latter material scrapes well without scratching the surface. I prefer to use a metal rib for scraping while the pot revolves on the wheel; before the surface slip is completely scraped away, the partially-scraped surface sometimes looks very nice and might be considered better than a cleanly-scraped background.

The pot is glazed after it has been bisque fired. A clear, colorless glaze is the obvious choice, and a thin-to-medium application gives the best result. In such a case, the clay and pot are the most important elements, not the glaze. A light-colored transparent glaze works very well also, and a celadon is excellent. A low-fire turquoise glaze, one similar to those used by the Persians over their black slip decorations, gives a handsome effect over white and brown or white and black designs. The Cone 06 transparent matt glazes are very good for this technique. Cone 10 reduction glazes do not have the good quality found in the low-fire transparents, and the translucent matts are perhaps the best for slip inlay work at the higher temperatures.

1. *Decorative buttons are used to impress a random pattern into the leather-hard clay.*

2. *Layers of thin slip are painted over the nearly-dry surface to completely fill the depressions.*

3. *When the slip is dry, the surface is scraped until only the stamped pattern is left colored.*

4. *Finished pot, glazed with transparent gray matt, appears dark brown against a pearl gray background.*

Slip Transfer with Paper

ONE OF THE VARIATIONS OF THE TRANSFER METHOD of decorating with colored clay slips or engobes involves dipping small pieces of paper into the slip, then transferring these to the surface of the pot in a random, mosaic-like pattern. The technique might be thought of as a crude decalcomania process except for the fact that only one-of-a-kind decorations are produced. The method is simple and requires no skill in drawing and painting.

A dry or nearly-dry piece of greenware is needed for this technique because the surface should be absorbent. A single color of slip can be used for decorating, or several different colors can be selected. Each color should be well mixed until it is smooth and thick. The paper for the transfer process might be a piece of newspaper, paper toweling, or wrapping paper; perhaps some of each could be used.

The paper is torn into narrow irregular strips, the best shape for a first attempt at this technique. One of the strips is dipped into the first color—perhaps white engobe—and this is pressed onto the greenware pot in a horizontal position. The paper is peeled away, leaving the slip on the absorbent clay, and the used paper is discarded. This process transfers white slip to the greenware pot in the shape of the torn paper, perhaps in an even more interesting shape. This unusual shape and the texture of the slip on the pot produce a unique character that could not be duplicated with a brush or by any other means.

The same process is repeated, transferring engobe on the paper to selected areas on the pot in order to make a pleasing spatial arrangement. If the pot is made from a red-firing clay, areas of the white slip alone would provide enough decorative treatment.

An additional color of slip could be used in the same manner, perhaps overlapping some of the white areas with strips of blue engobe. This might prove to be exciting enough, or still another color might be added. If a few strips of paper are dipped into rust-colored slip and transferred to the pot in an overlapping manner again, a new effect is produced. Some black slip could be added for a final color. Since this color is applied last, and because black is so dominant, perhaps the paper strips used for transferring it might be very narrow. If the original white slip has become so overlapped with other colors that its effectiveness is lost, strips of white might be added over some of the black.

Of course this process could be carried on and on, using more colors or applying the same colors over one another. The use of many applications and colors might even suggest a Jackson Pollock painting.

With one piece finished, another might be attempted using variations of some of the original elements. Long strips of paper dipped in slip might be arranged on the pot in vertical positions instead of horizontal ones. Diagonal placements are rather difficult and the results not really worth the time and effort expended. I would also suggest that strips of paper should not be crossed upon one another. At each intersection a new center of interest would be formed and the composition would suffer.

Another variation that can be attempted is the use of strips of paper of different sizes and shapes on a single pot. Paper also can be folded to produce some very interesting torn shapes. If the slip transfer decoration doesn't work out, some or all of it may be scratched off and another decoration substituted.

The best glaze for use over one of these transfer decorations in a colorless transparent one. The best result usually comes if it is applied in a thin coating; a thick application may result in an obscured decoration. A very light-colored transparent glaze might be very beautiful over some decorations, and there are various celadons, ambers, olive greens and cobalt blues that could give splendid results.

1. *Strips of newspaper are dipped into slip and pressed onto the nearly-dry pot to form a random pattern. When the paper is removed, the slip adheres to the pot.*

2. *More strips of paper are dipped into a second color of slip and pressed to the pot in a horizontal pattern. The various slip colors overlap one another.*

3. *White, blue, brown and black slips were used on the demonstration piece. After bisque firing, the bottle was glazed **with** a transparent gray matt.*

4. *Newspaper was torn into decorative patterns and dipped in rust and black engobe before transferring them to this vase. Glaze is a transparent gray matt.*

Slip Transfer with Cloth

WOVEN MATERIALS CAN BE DIPPED IN SLIP, attached to a clay form, allowed to dry and then fired. The textile burns away in the firing but the clay remains. When it is glazed it is quite strong, even though it looks fragile. This process is often used by hobbyists to festoon figurines with lace for a very realistic effect.

Art potters generally do not approve of lace-draped figures, but the technique is one that should not be ignored. A large, rugged pot can be embellished with slip-coated burlap, netting, string, cord or any other bold woven textiles. If the process is used judiciously, some very handsome pots may result.

The pottery form used for this decorating technique can be either a moist or dry one. Several pieces of burlap cloth are cut out, soaked in the clay slip, then applied to the greenware piece. The pieces of cloth must be so placed that they make an interesting pattern on the pot. A string or cord might also be dipped in the slip, then wrapped around the clay form to make an interesting linear design and integrate the design elements.

When the decoration is complete and the pot and slip are dry, the piece is bisque fired and then glazed. Because the decorative areas are extremely fragile in both the greenware and bisque stages, the pot must be handled gently.

Probably the best glaze for use on a pot decorated in this manner would be a transparent one, because it would reveal the cloth texture to its best advantage. An opaque glaze would conceal too much of the special decorative effect. Perhaps partially glazing the outside of the pot would be a good solution to this particular problem.

While some aspects of this technique are limited, it is a very challenging method of decorating and one that deserves some consideration by any potter who enjoys decorating.

1. Pieces of burlap are cut and dipped into a clay slip or engobe that offers some color contrast to the clay that was used for making the pot.

2. The slip-coated burlap is pressed against the pot; a small piece of potato-sacking is dipped in slip and pressed against the pot for a different effect.

3. Various shapes of coarse textiles are dipped in colored slip or engobe and attached to the pot to create a random-type of decoration.

4. A piece of rough string is coated with clay slip and wrapped around the pot in such a manner as to connect the various design elements.

5. After firing, the fabric has burned away, leaving a heavily textured decoration of white slip on a buff-colored clay. Firing was to Cone 10.

6. Stoneware planter was decorated by dipping potato sacking and string in white and black engobes. An interesting textural pattern results when the fabric is burned away in the firing.

Incised Line on Glaze

INCISED LINE DECORATION ON GLAZE is a simple and effective technique, one that can be used on bisque pottery without any previous preparation. Pieces made from red- or brown-burning clay give the best results from this technique; buff or white clays are not as effective. It is possible to stain a light-colored bisque pot with a darker color, and if this is done I would suggest that the inside of the piece be glazed first in order to avoid handling the outside surface of the pot, and possibly marring it, after the stain is applied.

A very satisfactory stain can be made by mixing some red iron oxide with quite a bit of water. Barnard clay can be used instead of iron and the effect would be similar. The easiest method of applying the stain is to center the piece (if it is a symmetrical one) on the potter's wheel or banding wheel, then paint the outer surface with the thin mixture. Either a brush or sponge can be used to apply a thin, even coating to the bisque. It is wise to avoid a heavy coating for several reasons. First, a heavy coating of iron would be ugly on the finished piece. Second, there is a possibility that too much iron might flux and dominate the glaze. Third, it may cause the glaze to crawl, a disagreeable defect.

The outside of the piece is glazed after the stain has been applied. If the pot is made from a dark-firing clay, it is not necessary to use the coating of stain, of course. The glaze selected must be one that does not flow or run in the firing. Usually a matt glaze is best for this technique, but a glossy opaque glaze can be used, just as long as it is one that will not become too fluid and run when the piece is fired. A transparent glaze would be almost completely useless for this particular decorating process.

It is best to incise the design through the glaze immediately after the glaze is applied, while it is still moist. If the glaze and pot are dry when the design is made, it is difficult to control the incising lines. Dry glaze has a tendency to chip from the surface and large areas may come off the pot.

A design may be sketched on the glaze surface with a soft lead pencil, a piece of soft charcoal, or brush and ink. Generally, however, it is preferable to sketch some ideas on paper first and then work freely on the pot, making any changes in the original plan as you progress.

1. A bisque bottle is sprayed with glaze. While the glaze is still wet, lines are scratched through to the bisque surface in a free "doodle" pattern.

2. Continuous lines are used to completely enclose the small design patterns being created. If the pot surface is well filled, the decorating result should be good.

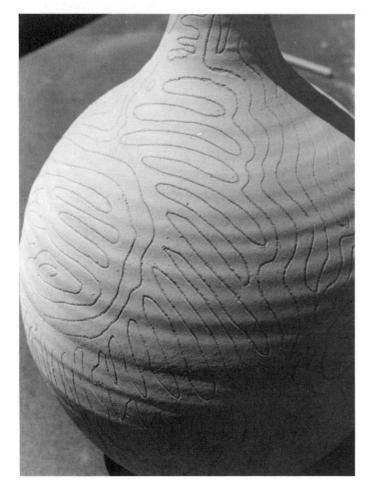

3. Close-up view shows the bottle surface after the incised line pattern is complete. The piece is ready for firing as soon as the pot and glaze are dry.

4. The edges of the scratched line are softened considerably after firing. The dark color of the clay (or stain) gives a good contrast to the light-colored glaze.

Red clay bottle was sprayed with a Waxy Tan Matt Glaze that had granular ilmenite added. Unfired glaze was scratched with a nail to produce a linear pattern, then fired to Cone 10.

Large pot made by throwing coils of clay as they were added. The unfired Waxy White Glaze was incised in a free "doodle" pattern, then fired to Cone 10 reduction.

Any kind of "doodle" pattern will work quite well for this kind of decoration. A good basic approach is to keep all lines anywhere from ¼ to ⅞ of an inch apart; this is important in creating an all-over effect. In addition, there is the possibility that the glaze between the lines may peel or chip off if the lines are too close together. There are times when this effect might be considered as an advantage, but generally it is looked upon as a defect.

The design may be started almost anywhere on the surface. A continuous line drawing is recommended because it usually produces an excellent effect. Small areas may also be completely enclosed by a continuous line for another good design pattern. Generally speaking, if the shapes created by the lines fill in the space, the end result of the decoration should be good.

One of the best tools for cutting through the glaze is the point of a medium-size nail. A very delicate line can be made with a needle point. Other pointed tools that work well are a dentist's probe, a crochet hook, or a knitting needle. The line is scratched through the glaze and down to the bisque surface.

When the design is finished and the pot and glaze are dry, the piece is fired. After firing, you will notice that the edges of the scratched lines are softened considerably. The dark color of the clay (or the stain) gives a good contrast if a light- or medium-colored glaze is used. If a dark glaze is used over a dark body or stain, the effect can be very subtle and beautiful.

You will find that this decorating technique works very nicely with most types of glazes, at any temperature, and in either an oxidation or reduction atmosphere. If the potter selects a glaze that won't run in the firing, and if he doesn't overfire the glaze, he should have no trouble with this decorating method.

Stoneware floor vase was glazed with white matt, then large areas of turquoise and cobalt matt were spotted on the surface with a large flat brush. A pattern was printed over this by dipping a natural sponge in wax and transferring it to the glaze. Iron oxide was painted over all, then a heavy wavy-line design was incised. Cone 10 reduction.

45

Wax Resist Printing

THE WAX RESIST TECHNIQUE is one of the most useful methods for decorating. It works very well for slip and it gives handsome results with glaze. It is a wonderful technique for potters with experience in drawing and painting; it also is an excellent decorating method for those with even very limited skill with the pencil and brush.

The best material for wax-resist decorating is a wax emulsion available under the name of *Ceremul "A."* Paraffin can be melted and used but it has some limitations that make it less desirable than the emulsion. For one thing, regular wax must be kept warm if it is to remain in a liquid stage for the potter-decorator's use; for another, it is very hard on brushes and sponges and necessitates cleaning them with a special solvent. Wax emulsion remains in the liquid stage and sponges and brushes used with it can be cleaned in water.

The wax-resist technique is done on dry, unfired glaze. A bisque pot is glazed inside and out with a light-colored glaze that will not flow or run in the firing. It is important that the outside glaze coating be as even as possible. I would recommend that a binder of some sort be added to the glaze to present a hard surface when the glaze is dry and ready for decorating. Gum tragacanth or gum arabic make wonderful binders but they sour without the addition of a preservative. CMC, a synthetic gum, can be used, as can Karo syrup. A tablespoon of the binder to a gallon of glaze should work very well. Decorating can be started when the glaze is dry.

The easiest method of producing a wax pattern or design on the pot is printing with a sponge. A large natural sponge is fine for producing a coarse-textured print and a smaller sponge is useful for obtaining a fine-textured print. By pressing the wax-coated sponge against the pot surface, an effect similar to block printing results.

The sponge is first soaked in water, then squeezed almost dry. The wax emulsion is poured into a bowl or pan and then a portion of the sponge is dipped into it. The sponge is rolled onto the dry glaze with a gentle motion to deposit a lacy print of wax. The printing is continued until the sponge pattern covers the pot or as much of it as is desired. If some larger, solid areas are needed, these can be painted in with a brush. The waxed areas will resist the next coating of color that is to be applied and remain the color of the base glaze coating after firing. Wash the sponge in water immediately after use.

Decorating is completed by centering the pot on the wheel and applying another color or glaze over the waxed surface. (When handling the pot, do not touch areas that are waxed, as the wax and glaze beneath will come off.) I would suggest mixing some red iron oxide with water to make a very thin wash of color. About one tablespoon of iron oxide to a cup of water should make an adequate mixture. A large brush is loaded with the wash and applied thinly and evenly to the wax-coated surface as the pot revolves on the wheel. The color soaks into the glaze wherever it is not protected by the wax, and this produces a handsome dark and light textured effect. The process can be repeated about three times in order to secure as even a coating as possible. No matter how carefully it is applied, the color will not give a uniform effect but it will be much better than a sloppy coating. I would caution against getting a very heavy application of iron because it may cause the glaze to run and even wrinkle; in addition, it will be black and ugly. If the coating is too thin, there will not be enough color for contrast. As in almost all ceramic work, it is necessary to experiment in order to learn just how the best results can be obtained. As soon as the glaze is dry and the piece can be handled, it is carefully lifted from the wheel and placed in the kiln for the final firing.

Interesting prints can be made by dipping a wad of yarn or string in wax and pressing this to the unfired glaze on a pot. Crushed newspaper, synthetic sponges, and chamois provide unique prints for decorating, too. Dry synthetic sponges can be cut into squares, circles and many other shapes and used for printing wax patterns. It is exciting to discover new decorating materials, so use your imagination when hunting for print-making devices.

1. A piece of natural sponge is dampened, then dipped in wax emulsion and pressed against the surface of an unfired glazed pot to give a textured print.

2. When waxing is complete, the pot is centered on the wheel and rotated while several coatings of a very thin red iron oxide and water mixture are brushed on the surface.

3. The iron oxide wash is not applied near the top because wax was not printed here. Instead, two bands of the colorant are used on the neck to give accent.

4. Bisque piece was glazed inside and out with White G-Matt-3 Glaze, given a wax-print decoration, then brushed with diluted red iron oxide and glaze fired.

Spatter Decoration with Wax

WAX CAN BE APPLIED TO A GLAZED, unfired pot in many unusual methods to produce very interesting decoratings. Two of these techniques that are especially good ones for the inexperienced decorator consist of spattering a design with wax, and "shooting" a decorative wax pattern on a glazed pot surface. These techniques are not only easy; they are fun!

Both techniques are done on a bisque pot that has been coated with a light-colored glaze. The glaze should be dry and hard but not yet fired. Wax emulsion (*Ceremul "A"*) is used for both of these decorating methods.

Spattering is done by selecting a large brush, loading it with thick, undiluted wax emulsion, then "throwing" the wax from the brush onto the pot. It is difficult to describe this procedure, but it is easy to do and any potter should be able to develop interesting patterns with no trouble at all.

Because this technique can result in wax getting on things other than the pot, it may be done out of doors in good weather. If the first decorating attempts are not satisfactory, the wax and glaze can be scraped and washed from the pot surface so that a new start can be made. If wax gets on the clay itself, it can be removed by heating the pot in the kiln or an oven to about 300°F in order to burn off the wax.

An altogether different type of accidental wax pattern can be made by filling a child's water pistol with wax resist emulsion and "shooting" or squirting a design pattern on the unfired glaze surface. As with the other informal methods of applying wax, this one may require a bit of practice before a semi-controlled effect is achieved.

If decorating work is being done against a white glaze and it is difficult to see just where the wax is, the wax emulsion can be colored with ink. The ink burns away in the firing.

Decorating is completed by placing the pot on the wheel and centering it, then brushing on a coating of oxide diluted with water, as described in the preceding project.

Red iron oxide is the best pigment to use with this technique. It gives different colors when used with different glazes, and varies in effect when used in lighter or heavier coatings on the same glaze. Each base glaze reacts differently to iron when it is used on the surface. With White G-Matt-3 Glaze, it is often quite orange in color. With White Waxy Glaze, it gives amber to brown. A wax resist pattern over even a dark glaze, with iron oxide brushed on, can give a rich effect. If the Transparent Brown Chun Glaze is used on the base glaze, the design will be transparent brown against a background of opaque rust red.

Other colorants may be used instead of iron for the wash over a wax-resist decoration. Cobalt oxide or cobalt carbonate may be thinned with water and used, but because cobalt is a very strong pigment, it must be applied very thinly. If the glaze being used gives a beautiful blue when colored with cobalt, it will be good for use with this technique. Generally, cobalt gives the best color when used in high zinc glazes; avoid high magnesium glazes, such as White Waxy Glaze, because an unattractive mauve results.

It is possible to use some underglazes thinned with water, too. I have gotten good results with thinned black underglaze applied in a medium coating. It should not be as heavy as iron nor should it be as light as a cobalt application. I would strongly recommend that some tests be made by painting various oxides and underglaze colors on different base glazes and firing them for permanent records of the results.

1. Wax is spattered from a large brush onto a dry unfired glaze to obtain a part-accidental, part-controlled decoration. Wax is colored with ink which will burn out in the firing.

2. Because of the nature of the application, it may be desirable to do this technique out of doors or in an area that doesn't need to be cleaned.

3. The piece is centered on the wheel and a thin mixture of red iron oxide and water is brushed over the wax and glaze. Waxed areas resist the added colorant.

4. Finished piece after firing to Cone 10 reduction. Base glaze was White Waxy Matt; the top wash over the wax was red iron oxide thinned with water.

5. Partially-controlled decoration is applied by shooting or squirting wax from a toy water pistol onto the dry, unfired base glaze (White Waxy Matt).

6. The pot is centered on the wheel and rotated while thinned red iron oxide is brushed over the wax and base glaze from a large, fully-charged brush.

7. After firing to Cone 10 in a reduction atmosphere, the areas covered with wax are white; areas not covered range from amber to brown, depending on thickness of the iron wash.

8. Decoration on this vase was wax spattered from a brush. Base glaze was White G-Matt-3; wash over the wax decoration was water-diluted red iron oxide.

Poured Patterns in Glaze

ONE OF THE EASIEST METHODS of enhancing the surface of a piece of pottery is by applying the glaze in a decorative manner. While there are several ways in which this can be done, the most effective technique is that of pouring the glaze onto the outer surface.

When using this decorating technique it is best to glaze the inside of the bisque pot first, particularly if it is a vertical shape. If this is done after the outside has been decorated, there is a chance that the inside glaze may dribble over the decoration when it is poured out of the bisque pot.

If the surface is just to be partially glazed, and the clay body is too light in color to offer enough contrast to the glaze, the body can be tinted by sponging or brushing red iron oxide or Barnard clay onto the pot, then partially wiping it off. To do this, center the pot on the wheel, start the wheel rotating, then sponge or brush an even coating of the color over the outside of the piece.

If the pot is to be partially glazed, choose a glaze that contrasts nicely with the color of the clay. If a dark clay is used, it probably would be best to refrain from using a brown glaze. The glaze, which should be a little thicker than usual, can be put in a pitcher or some other spouted container for easy pouring.

A good arrangement for supporting a pot when it is poured consists of a large bowl or dish pan with two sticks placed across it in parallel fashion. The sticks support the pot, and the bowl or pan catches the excess glaze as it flows from the piece.

The pot is placed upright on the sticks and supported on the back side with one hand; the other hand is used to pour the glaze from the pitcher. I would suggest placing the lip of the pitcher about two-thirds or three-quarters of the way up the pot, quickly pouring a generous amount of glaze against the surface, then rapidly withdrawing the pitcher. As the pitcher is pulled away, a drop of glaze will run down the wall. When this technique is used on a swelling form, a generous application of glaze will produce a large oval or horseshoe pattern.

The pot is turned around now and the process repeated on the opposite side. This may be enough, or it may be necessary to repeat the pouring between the initial two decorative areas, either using the same glaze or a different one. If a different glaze is used, another pan and stick arrangement must be provided for this pouring.

Variations on this simple pouring technique include overlapping the poured patterns, either with one glaze or with two different ones; using larger and smaller poured patterns; and varying the placement of the patterns on the surface. A smaller poured pattern used lower and inside a larger pattern very often can be quite beautiful.

A variety of patterns can be produced by using different vessels for the pouring. These include pitchers with wider or smaller spouts, watering cans, oil cans, and teapots. If the potter is very fond of this decorating technique he may want to throw a series of pitchers with special pouring spouts for this purpose.

Glaze pouring can be done simply by holding the bisque pot over a pan and pouring glaze from a cup or pitcher. The advantage of this method is that the pot can be held in almost any position, right-side-up, upside-down, or at a slant; it can even be moved while the glaze is poured on the surface. When this technique is used, the glaze should be fairly thick and each area should be poured only once.

It is easy to over-decorate by this method. While one glaze can be quite beautiful when poured over another color, too many different colors can give very disappointing results. I would also caution against attempting to "paint on" a poured design because it is almost certain to betray its technique.

It may take a little practice to use either of the above techniques skillfully. When one can pour with some knowledge of how the glaze will react, the process can be done easily, quickly and in a very relaxed manner. Until the potter can produce good effects by pouring, any unsuccessful attempts can be salvaged by washing the glaze from the pot, drying the bisque, and starting over again.

1. A bisque pot is glazed inside, then supported on sticks over a pan for the pouring process. A pitcher is used to pour large patterns of glaze on the pot surface.

2. Smaller patterns are poured in a lower position over the large initial patterns. The back side of the bottle is supported by the hand while the glaze is poured.

3. Color contrast was achieved here by pouring a glaze pattern in blue green over a pot that was first completely glazed **with** a white waxy matt.

4. This red clay vase was decorated by holding it in one hand at an angle and pouring a translucent tan matt glaze in a random pattern.

Decorative Glaze Dipping

DIPPING A POT IN GLAZE is another quick and effective method of decoration. The dipping process is used commercially to glaze ceramic dinnerware, but this is done to give the pieces a single covering glaze and not for any special decorative effects.

Decorative dipping can be done in many combinations to achieve a tremendous number of different colors, patterns and textures. To mention just a few, a plate can be completely dipped in white glaze, allowed to dry, and then just about a third of it dipped into another color of glaze; two-thirds of a plate may be dipped in one glaze and the remaining third dipped in a contrasting color of glaze so that the two glazes overlap; a plate can be completely glazed in one color and the edges dipped evenly in fifths to create a star pattern around the rim; a plate might be dipped halfway into a translucent white waxy glaze, then be rotated one-fifth and dipped again, repeating this process until another star pattern is produced by single and double thicknesses of one glaze. This last pattern is particularly subtle because of the varying degrees of whiteness produced with the translucent glaze.

A pitcher shape can be glazed inside and out at the same time by dipping half of it for the spout section, and again for the handle side. If the dipping is done at an angle, the effect can be quite beautiful with either one glaze or two different ones.

Interesting effects can be given cylindrical forms by holding them in a horizontal position and dipping a portion of the inside and out at the same time. To obtain even dipping marks each time, the glaze can be put into a shallow pan. A cake pan can be used and filled with half an inch or an inch of glaze. The pot is held by the neck and foot and dipped into the glaze until it touches the bottom of the pan, then it is lifted out and held for about ten seconds. Next, it is revolved in the hands so that the opposite side is in position for dipping, then it is dipped into the glaze. This can be repeated until the whole pot is dipped. Each time the pot is dipped, it is allowed to touch the bottom; in this way each dip pattern will be the same. Any variation in the pot shape itself will add to the effectiveness of the pattern produced by the dipping technique.

Double dipping produces some beautiful results also, and a bottle shape is excellent for this technique. The bottle is glazed inside and out with a single glaze, then the rounded cheek of the form is dipped into a shallow pan of a different glaze in three, four or five sections to produce rounded patches of glaze on top of the base glaze. Many times the underneath glaze will bubble up through the top glaze in the firing and produce a speckled texture.

Another type of dipping involves holding a pot horizontally and dipping it half way into a glaze, removing it and rotating it a third of the way around, then dipping it half way into a second color, and repeating the whole process with still a third color. Because each color shows and each color overlaps another, the effect can be a very exciting one.

It is extremely important to stir the glaze frequently when pieces are being decorated by the dipping method. When glaze stands, heavy particles settle to the bottom of the container. If a pot is dipped into a glaze that hasn't been stirred just before use, an incomplete job will result. I have found that a wire whisk is excellent for stirring, and I have one available for each color of glaze I am using.

If a number of large pots are to be glazed, practically a whole kiln-full can be dip-decorated in a very short time and each pot will have an individual appearance. Five different glazes are prepared and each one is placed in a large container, such as a baby bathtub. If an assistant can be found, he can stir each glaze just before it is to be used, and clean the foot-rims of the glazed pots. The glazing process consists of holding a large vase horizontally, by the neck and foot, and plunging it into the first glaze to cover about a third or half of the surface. As soon as it comes from this glaze, it is rotated slightly and dipped into the next glaze, and so on until from three to five colors have been incorporated into an effective pattern.

53

Top left: Cake pans or photography trays can be used to obtain just the right amount and proper depth of glaze needed for the decorative dipping process.

Top right: The shape of a pot governs, to a certain extent, the decorative effects possible when pieces of bisque are dipped in glaze to decorate them.

Above: These three bottles are different, yet they have a related feeling because the same glazes and dipping techniques were used on each one.

Right: The stoneware bottle was dipped in an overlapping pattern in several different glazes. Its strong shape affected the resulting patterns of glaze.

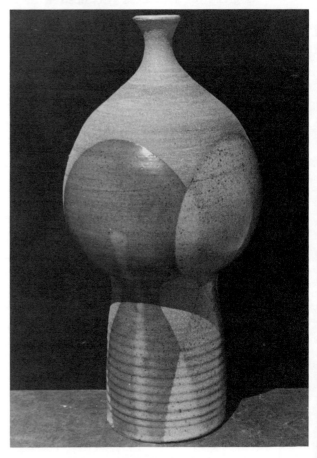

Plastic garbage cans make excellent storage bins for large amounts of glaze. A wooden platform can be built and equipped with casters to provide a mobile base for each container of glaze. These can be used effectively for completely dipping the outside of a large pot in one glaze. After the glaze is thoroughly stirred, the pot is held right-side-up and plunged into the glaze almost to the rim. It is removed and allowed to dry, then it is inverted and the top is dipped twice to deposit a thick rim of glaze at the lip. This makes a very fine effect after firing.

Dipping tongs can be purchased for dipping smaller pots. If these are used, it is important to remember that the pot should be removed from the glaze at the same angle at which it was inserted. Any attempt to lift the piece while it is full of glaze may result in the breaking of a piece of the bisque at its rim.

Crackle Glaze as Decoration

AN EFFECTIVE BUT SIMPLE METHOD of decorating a piece of pottery is through the use of a crackle glaze. The breaks or fissures that develop in a glaze were called "craquel' by the French and it is from this word that we have our term *crackle* as a method of decorating a pottery surface. The words "crackle" and "craze" often are confusing and a definition is in order here.

When a glaze cracks or crazes on a pot, and the crackle is colored to give it emphasis, it is considered as a decorative treatment and a desirable effect. When a glaze crazes and the potter doesn't want this effect, the glaze is considered defective. While this seems to constitute the main difference between crackle and craze, there is much more that can be said about them.

When a glaze crazes on a *vitrified* body, there is very little harm done. When a glaze crazes on a *porous* body, the resulting piece must be considered a poor one. Liquids used in or on such a piece can soak through the crack lines of the glaze and saturate the body. A vase would leak water and its saturated wet foot could ruin furniture. Because food and grease can lodge in the craze lines of a glaze on an absorbent clay dish, such a piece would be unsanitary.

When the clay is vitreous, as in stoneware, china or porcelain, there isn't much trouble from a crazed glaze. The pot won't leak and the clay won't soak up any liquids. Food or grease might remain within the crackle, but this is about all.

From a sanitary standpoint, dishes, bowls, cups and casseroles should not have crackle or crazed glazes. If a housewife buys a set of commercial dishes and some of the pieces craze or crackle, she can, and probably will, return the defective pieces and get replacements. The same housewife might buy an inexpensive Mexican pottery bowl for its charm and overlook the fact that its glaze is not only crazed but also is probably a toxic one.

All glazes will craze if the clay bodies on which they are used are not fired high enough to mature them. If the clay body is mature, it is rather difficult to find a glaze that will craze consistently and in a pleasing pattern. A thin layer of glaze does not develop a crackle as easily as a thick coating. A thinner layer generally gives a smaller crackle pattern than a thicker coating of the same glaze.

The one ingredient that is more likely to induce crazing in a glaze more than any other material is sodium. If nepheline syenite is substituted for feldspar in a glaze, it also may induce crazing. Crazing might be approached through the clay. Some additional kaolin can be wedged into a stoneware body in order to make it slightly immature for use at the normal firing temperature and thus induce crazing. Firing procedure can aid in producing a crazed glaze, for a very fast cooling can start the crazing process.

If a low-fire glaze is used on a high-fired body to get a crackle glaze, the finished pot can be made waterproof by the simple process of soaking it overnight in skimmed milk, then allowing the piece to stand unwashed for about a week. The milk soaks into the pores of the clay, sours, dries, and fills the porous body with a casein glue. The new acrylic paints also can be used to waterproof crackle-glazed pieces. Clear, colorless acrylic can be diluted with water, poured into a piece, and allowed to soak through the crackle and into the body. When the liquid is poured out, the pot can be wiped clean and dry and it should prove to be waterproof.

On an immature body, a crackle usually has comparatively wide fissures. The fissures generally are close together on a crackle glaze used on a vitreous body. When the fissures are large, it is a simple job to rub pigment into them for coloring. Such a crackle is decorative and usually quite fascinating.

Potters in China during the Sung dynasty started the practice of coloring crackle glazes for decorative effects, and the practice has continued until the present day. Materials that can be used for staining a crackle glaze include shoe polish, India ink, and oil colors diluted with turpentine. Dark, earthy colors are best for coloring crackle lines; however, bright colors such as red or green can be used for an effect that is interesting but rather gaudy. If a pot is to be rubbed with any pigment to bring out the crackle, the piece should not be handled much with the bare hands because oils from the hands can fill the fissures and thereby ruin the possibility of a good all-over pattern.

When a pot with a crackle glaze comes hot from the kiln, it can be colored immediately with a black pigment to give it a large, bold decorative effect. For about a week longer the glaze will continue to craze; if you have the piece in your room at night when all is still, you may hear the glaze give a tinkling sound as it crazes. (Perhaps this is what Omer Khayyam meant when he wrote in his "Rubaiyat" about pots talking to each other.) This additional crackle will be in a smaller pattern, and if it is stained in a different color—perhaps a brown—it will make an interesting contrast with the bolder black lines. This was a decorative device used by the ancient Chinese potters.

The Chinese also pioneered in the *control* of crackle glazes. They could achieve a large crackle called "crab's claw" and a very small pattern named "fish roe," as well as many others. They devised glazes that crackled in square patterns, angular ones, and rounded octagon-shaped patterns. Today some of the Royal Copenhagen porcelain depends on a minute crackle pattern for its decoration.

Some stoneware glazes, among them the celadons, have crazed lines that are so fine and fit so closely together that pigment as refined as oil paint cannot be rubbed into them. Only a dye will go into these cracks, and dyes are weak in coloring power and have a tendency to fade. One technique for coloring such crackle involves working with sulphuric acid. This is effective but necessitates much care on the part of the potter in handling the material. An amount of the acid is diluted with eight parts of water; to this is added some sugar to make a saturated solution. The pot is soaked in this solution for about one minute, then the surface is carefully wiped clean. After this, the pot is placed in the kitchen oven and heated to about 300 degrees. The sugar turns to carbon and gives the crackle lines a very beautiful black color.

In addition to the use of oil paints, stains or dyes for coloring crackle, ceramic under-glaze colors can be used. When this material is used, pots can be refired to give a permanent stain to the glaze. If the glaze is fired slightly higher than the first firing, it will flow slightly and blur the crackle pattern or give it a lacy effect. This could be done over and over to develop some really unusual effects.

If a crackle glaze with no color added is refired just to the point of softening of the glaze (about 1300°), the edges of the crackle will melt first. If the firing is stopped here, the crackle pattern will have an incised appearance that is quite fascinating.

Another experiment involves the use of a saturated solution of some soluble salt, such as copper sulphate or cobalt nitrate. If the crackle-glaze pot is soaked in this solution for about ten seconds, the solution should run into the crackle and stain the clay body beneath. When this pot is refired to bring out the color, still another unique effect is obtained. These are just a few of the variations for using crackle glaze for decorative effects. As the potter works with these, he will come up with many new ideas of his own for experimentation.

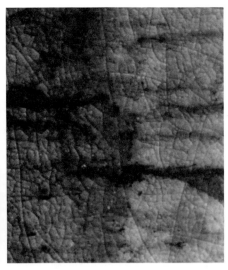

Close-up view of a crackle glaze that has been stained. Note the much smaller crackle pattern that developed after the first crackle lines were colored.

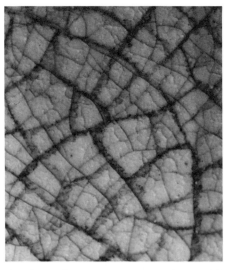

Small crackle pattern was stained with black underglaze, then refired to a higher temperature to blur the crackle. New crackle was colored with brown pigment.

Large crackle was colored with copper carbonate and refired. After a fine network of new lines appeared, the piece was refired to produce an incised crackle.

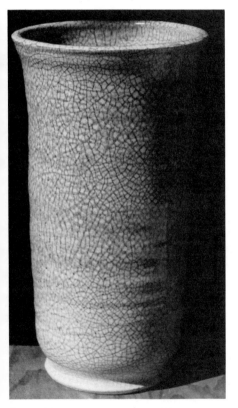

Jar with a very small crackle pattern.

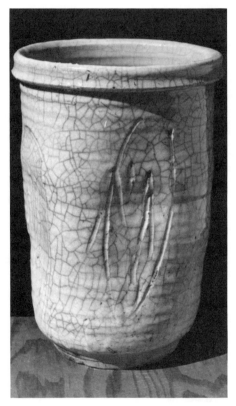

Jar with a medium-size crackle pattern.

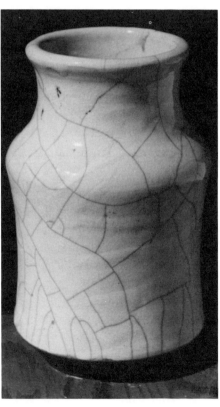

Vase with a very large crackle pattern.

Crater Glaze Textures

THE CRATERS ON THE MOON'S SURFACE have excited man's imagination for many years and they are of particular interest in our own time of space exploration. The potter has long had in his repertory of glazes an effect that resembles the lunar surface, one created by using a glaze that foams and bubbles to create craters or one that has a crusty appearance similar to lava. Both of these are very decorative but they are somewhat limited in color range. Because they are difficult to achieve, the potter must be prepared to spend considerable time experimenting with the glazes themselves, thickness of application, and firing.

One glaze that gives a rather good effect for Cone 10 reduction firing is a low-fire raku glaze that we accidentally fired with some high temperature glazes. It came out of the kiln a foamy, bubbly mess, with large patches of green against a gray background. We used a piece of broken kiln shelf to break the bubbles and grind away the sharp edges, and then the glaze had the appearance of "craters on the moon." The glaze name is "Raku Crater Glaze," and its formula, as well as the formulas for the other glazes mentioned here, can be found in the last section of this handbook. This glaze has excellent decorative possibilities, especially with other colorants in place of the chromium oxide. Perhaps a Cone 10 matt glaze could be used in a light application over it.

A wonderful crater effect for Cone 6 oxidation firing can be made by using "Albany Slip Glaze" as a base glaze. This glaze gives a clear, glossy medium-brown color, a good "little brown jug" effect. It can be made darker by increasing the red iron to about 2.6%, or by adding 0.5% of cobalt oxide. Another interesting effect can be had by adding 5.0% of tin oxide. No matter which of these variations you use, the glaze will be smooth and glossy, with no hint of any bubbling. However, all slip glazes will boil and bubble when they start to melt, which usually is from Cones 2 to 5. In a normal firing the bubbles smooth out to give a normal-appearing glaze. To keep the bubbled effect, "G.S. Matt Glaze", an ivory-white glaze, can be used over it. This is a dry matt by itself, with good but limited results.

To achieve the crater glaze effect with these two glazes, a medium application of the Albany Slip Glaze is first put on the pot. I have found that it is best to add some binder—a gum solution or corn syrup—to this glaze. Next, the G.S. Matt Glaze is applied over the slip glaze. Spraying is the best way to apply one glaze over another. When the glaze and pot are dry, they are fired in the Cone 3 to 6 range. The Albany Slip Glaze bubbles up through the ivory matt and creates large and small craters. If any blisters remain on the surface, they can be ground off very easily with a piece of kiln shelf; the result should be good.

Thickness of application is important in obtaining good texture. If either glaze is too thin, the craters may not develop. Firing is important too. At Cone 3 or 4, the bubbles usually are best; at Cone 6 they start smoothing out and the result is more "curdle" than "crater."

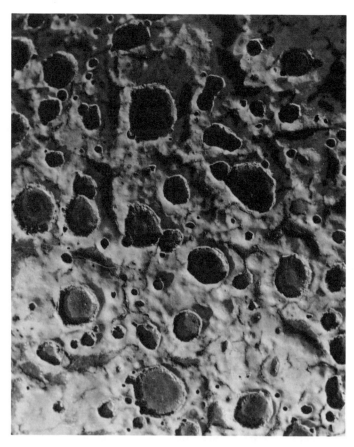

1. Albany Slip Glaze was first sprayed on this stoneware vase, then ivory colored G. S. Matt was sprayed on top of it. When dry, the piece was fired to Cone 5 oxidation.

2. Close-up of bubbled glaze shows the "craters on the moon" effect achieved by applying a white matt glaze over a glossy slip glaze.

3. Raku glaze, used on stoneware and fired to Cone 10 reduction, produced a blistered surface that was ground down with a piece of kiln shelf.

Slips and Engobes

THE TERMS "colored clay slips" and "engobes" are synonymous. A colored clay slip is to all intents and purposes the same as an engobe and vice versa. There are as many compositions of colored slips or engobes as there are potters. In general, the best engobe to use is one made of the same clay as that used to make the pot—with appropriate color and water added to make it into a slip. By following this practice, the problem of fitting the slip to the body is eliminated.

Each kind of clay acts a little different from any other and each clay shrinks differently, so it is quite a task to find one kind of clay that will make a satisfactory engobe for use on another kind of clay. This is especially true if one is seeking a white-clay engobe for a red clay pot.

The easiest solution is to use a buff body; or use a buff clay in the body and color it if the buff color isn't satisfactory. Then the buff clay can be the lightest color in the clay slip and coloring oxides can be added. The lighter colors such as yellow, light blue and light green will look well with a buff clay as the base of the slip, but they would not be good if a red-clay base were used instead for the engobe. There is no problem of the engobe's fitting the clay body because the clay for the engobe is the same as that used for the pot: both will shrink equally during drying and firing.

If it is necessary to make a white engobe which will fit a red clay, there are several ways of going about it. First, try all the white and light-buff clays available to you; make slips of them and put them on the red clay; fire and glaze the tests. Perhaps one of these white clays will fit and your difficulties will be over. If none of them fit, try the engobes suggested later in this article to see if any of them will do what you wish. And if that fails,

choose from among your tests the white clay that came the closest to fitting the red clay and adjust it to fit.

There are materials which can be added to the white clay to cut down its shrinkage, and other materials which will make it shrink even more. Choose a single material or a combination that will make your clay fit.

White clays, each having more or less shrinking capacity, can be added. Kaolins will not shrink much; plastic kaolins will shrink a bit more. Ball clays will shrink a good deal, some of them more than others; and bentonite will shrink very much—probably too much.

Flint is one of the materials which will keep your clay from shrinking as much as it ordinarily would by itself. Fine grog would work the same way but would not be as good an ingredient to use. Feldspar counteracts drying shrinkage but increases firing shrinkage.

The appropriate material, depending on whether you want to increase or counteract shrinkage, should be added to the white clay of the engobe in percentage quantities. For example, if a kaolin is being used for the base material and it doesn't shrink enough, a ball clay could be added in varying amounts—let's say, 5, 10, 15, 20 and 25%. After making and firing tests, you should have an engobe which comes closer to fitting; another series of similar tests should completely solve the problem.

If a ball clay is being used as the base material for the engobe and it shrinks too much, run a series of tests with flint added in varying amounts ranging from 5% through 25%. When these tests have been fired with a glaze over them there should be one which is so very close to fitting that it can easily be corrected.

The addition of 5% of powdered borax to your engobe can help it to fit. Borax is soluble; when a slip containing it is painted on a pot and the slip and pot dry, the borax sets up a thin skin of borax crystals between the surface of the pot and the engobe and this helps the engobe to adhere. During firing, the borax fuses first and produces a sticky layer of material between the body and the engobe, in this way helping to hold the engobe on the pot in and after firing.

Many stoneware bodies are dark in color. Such bodies give some of the most beautiful of effects, especially when decorated with engobes. Dark clay calls for a light-colored engobe; usually a potter has one that will fit his dark stoneware clay—an engobe that is quite white because of the ball clay and China clay in it.

If such an engobe is applied heavily, it stays white through the glaze firing. But many artist-potters would wish to decorate the pot with direct single brush strokes of the white slip—and this is a highly effective way of enriching the surface. A nice, thick transparent glaze over such a pot *should* be beautiful but frequently the design disappears in the firing and the potter's time has been wasted.

A white-clay-slip design will not disappear nearly as much if a transparent glaze is applied *very thinly* over the pot. There is a disadvantage, however, in using a thin layer of transparent glaze. The pot when fired appears to have been varnished; the beauty that goes with a thick glaze is lost.

This, I think, is what happens: when the glaze is molten in the kiln it dissolves some of the alumina and silica out of the body of the pot and some of the surface of the pot goes into the molten glass of the glaze. If, perchance, the surface of the pot has a nicely painted engobe decoration, it too is absorbed into the glaze and disappears from sight. There may be other or additional reasons for clay slip to lose its opacity, but the important thing is that it does tend to disappear under a glaze, especially at stoneware temperatures.

This "fault" in your engobe or clay slip may be corrected by the addition of some of your favorite zirconium opacifier. It is possible to add 50% of zirconium to a batch of engobe and this is the percentage I prefer. Make tests by adding five different amounts of zirconium oxide to your engobe. For the first test, add 10%; the second, 20%; then 30, 40 and 50%; and brush the five engobes on a pot. Try several transparent glazes over them to see which engobe is the most desirable and dependable.

A zirconium opacifier works very well in most engobes without disturbing the fit and the clay slip remains white under a thick layer of transparent glaze. Because of this, a white engobe can be brushed in single strokes over a dark clay body, in a beautiful decorative manner, and the glazing and firing in an oxidation or reduction atmosphere will not ordinarily destroy the design.

To make an engobe handle in a better way, to make it flow from the brush in a more silky fashion, a little glycerine can be added to the engobe. If you find glycerine too expensive or difficult to obtain, try some corn syrup or honey in the slip—either will improve its painting quality.

The following are some of the base engobes which can be used on stoneware:

White Engobe #1
(Cones 6-11)

Edgar Plastic Kaolin	34.0%
Feldspar	17.0
Flint	17.0
Bentonite	3.4
Zircopax	28.6
	100.0%

White Engobe #2
(Cones 6-11)

Nepheline Syenite	20%
Kaolin	25
Ball Clay	20
Flint	30
Borax	5
	100%

White Engobe #3
(Cones 6-11)

Edgar Plastic Kaolin	25%
Imperial Ball Clay	20
F4 Feldspar	20
Flint	30
Borax	5
	100%

The following engobes are very versatile. They can be used for earthenware as well as stoneware since their range extends from Cones 04 to 9

Engobe #4
(Cones 04-9)

Feldspar	12%
Flint	8
China Clay	80
	100%

Engobe #5
(Cones 04-9)

Kentucky Ball Clay	16%
Feldspar	30
Magnesium Carbonate	4
Flint	50
	100%

Engobe #6
(Cones 04-9)

Feldspar	10%
Talc	10
Ball Clay	20
Kaolin	30
Flint	25
Borax	5
	100%

Some suggestions for adding colors to slips or engobes are given below. Nearly all these colors are good for both oxidation and reduction firing:

20% Red Iron Oxide gives a good iron red

25% Red Iron Oxide plus 5% Manganese Dioxide gives a brown-black

10% Manganese Dioxide gives a brown

40% Barnard Clay gives brown (similar to above)

10% Black underglaze gives blue-black or green-black

1% Black Cobalt Oxide gives medium blue

2% Black Cobalt Oxide plus 3% Red Iron Oxide gives a strong blue

2% Red Iron Oxide plus ½% black Cobalt Oxide plus ½% Black Cobalt Oxide plus ½% Green Chromium Oxide gives a strong blue-green

It is possible to add quite a number of colors to this list by using glaze stains produced by various manufacturing companies which make ceramic colorants. From 10% to 20% of a glaze stain is usually effective.

To prepare the engobes, first weigh the dry ingredients, then add to them enough water to make a creamy slip. Stir this slip by hand; screen the slip first through a 30- or 40-mesh screen, then through an 80- or 100-mesh screen—perhaps twice through the 100-mesh. The process mixes the slip well and makes it smooth, and this is sufficient for an art potter. A slip *can* be processed to a greater extent. If the mixture is put in a ball mill the result will be very satisfactory.

The consistency of slip is controlled by the amount of water used in mixing the batch. The art potter will vary it to suit his purpose, depending on the decorative technique used. A slip can be deflocculated to make it thin or flocculated to make it thick, but it is better to add or subtract water for the desired consistency.

The chief controlling factors for the colors you can obtain from commercial stains are the glaze used and the temperature to which it is fired. A thorough testing of clay, engobe colors and glazes, in the potter's workshop, is the only reliable way of developing good colored engobes.

For working up a good palette of engobes the following test is suggested. Make several 6" x 10" tiles, ⅜-inch thick. Paint an inch-wide band of engobe the full 10-inch length of the tile and repeat with each color being tested; the number, name or any other information you wish to note may be scratched through each band of color. After the tile is bisque fired, apply various glazes in strips two inches wide *across* the bands of slip. Each glaze can be identified with a black underglaze pencil. When the tile has been fired to the proper cone, you will know which colors will work and the strength with which they will show through glaze. Some glazes will be good over some colors while other colors will be changed or destroyed by the glaze. A very few glazes will be quite good with all colors.

Glaze Recipes

THE GLAZE RECIPES listed here have worked very well over a number of years in my own work and in that of my students. No single glaze seems to perform exactly the same for everyone, however; a glaze that is considered wonderful by one potter may be thought of as poor by another craftsman. Each person must test, then accept, reject, or change the recipe until it fits his needs. The following glazes should give the ceramist a head start in the search for a formulary.

WAXY MATT GLAZE
(Cones 9-10)

Feldspar	41%
Gerstley Borate (Colemanite)	12
Dolomite	7
Talc	15
Kaolin	5
Flint	20
	100%

This is a beautiful semi-matt glaze that is translucent when used in a thin application. It is translucent and opalescent if overfired to Cone 11. This glaze is excellent for both reduction and oxidation firing. For colors in reduction firing, add the following:

1.0% Turquoise Glaze Stain for pale blue
2.0% Powdered Ilmenite and a pinch of Granular Ilmenite for oatmeal
3.0% to 5% Black Glaze Stain for black
5.0% Red Iron Oxide for brown
0.5% Cobalt Oxide for violet-blue

CHUN GLAZE
(Cones 9-10)

Feldspar	42.1%
Kaolin	1.8
Flint	27.2
Whiting	2.6
Gerstley Borate (Colemanite)	8.8
Dolomite	8.8
Zinc Oxide	1.7
Barium Carbonate	4.4
Tin Oxide	2.6
	100.0%

This is a good all-around glaze that is translucent at Cone 9 and clear at Cone 10. Specifically designed for reduction firing, the glaze can be used for oxidation if the tin oxide is omitted. For colors add the following:

2.0% Red Iron Oxide for celadon
4.0% Red Iron Oxide for dark celadon
6.0% Red Iron Oxide for dark brown
0.5% Copper Carbonate for copper red
2.0% Red Iron Oxide and 0.5% Cobalt Oxide for blue
4.0% Rutile and 0.5% Copper Carbonate for mottled blue
1.5% Green Chromium Oxide for chrome green

TRANSPARENT GRAY MATT
(Cone 10)

Nepheline Syenite	37%
Dolomite	15
Whiting	8
Kaolin	23
Flint	12
Zinc Oxide	2
Opax	3
	100%

This glaze is about as transparent as a good matt can be. It works well over engobes and gives a good effect with cobalt decoration. It may craze on some bodies, however.

G-MATT-3 GLAZE
(Cones 10-11)

Feldspar	50.0%
Whiting	8.5
Zinc Oxide	7.7
Barium Carbonate	20.6
Ball Clay	9.4
Rutile	3.8
	100.0%

A good glaze that usually gives a mottled effect, G-Matt-3 is dry at Cone 9½ (on thin application) and waxy at Cone 11 (on thick application). It is excellent for porcelain at Cone 11 oxidation firing. Colors recommended are as follows:

3.0% Copper Carbonate for green
1.5% Copper Carbonate for turquoise
2.0% Red Iron Oxide for tan
5.0% Red Iron Oxide for brown
1.5% Cobalt Oxide for cobalt blue
1.5% Black Nickel Oxide and 0.25% Chromium Oxide for olive green.

K.C.N.S.T. OPAQUE GLAZE
(Cones 8-10)

Feldspar	56.5%
Whiting	7.0
Kaolin	4.5
Flint	23.0
Red Iron Oxide	9.0
	100.0%

This is a saturated iron glaze with minute crystals in it that sparkle. On thin application it is brown; a thick coating gives a brown-black.

BROWN-BLACK OPAQUE GLAZE
(Cone 10)

Feldspar	42%
Whiting	16
Zinc Oxide	2
Kaolin	12
Flint	20
Iron Oxide	8
	100%

This is a shiny glaze that has a thick dark brown color when thickly applied and a medium-brown color when it is thin.

WAXY MATT REDUCTION
(Cone 10)

Feldspar	41.4%
Flint	21.8
Kaolin	10.3
Dolomite	9.8
Talc	12.1
Gerstley Borate (Colemanite)	4.6
	100.0%

An excellent glaze. For color additions, follow the suggestions listed under the Waxy Matt Glaze. A beautiful and unusual violet-blue color can be made by the addition of about 2% cobalt oxide.

LIGHT TAN CRYSTALLINE GLAZE
(Cones 8-10)

Feldspar	16.6%
Flint	25.1
Rutile	12.3
Whiting	6.0
Zinc Oxide	6.0
Red Lead	34.0
	100.0%

This is a textured glaze that works well on a fine body such as porcelain. Effects vary depending on the thickness of glaze application and the firing.

ALBANY SLIP GLAZE
(Cone 6)

Albany Slip Clay	55.4%
Red Lead	17.2
Cornwall Stone	8.1
Flint	8.0
Kaolin	3.2
Whiting	2.9
Zinc Oxide	1.3
Manganese Dioxide	2.6
Red Iron Oxide	.5
	99.2%

This glaze gives a clear, glossy medium-brown color.

RAKU CRATER GLAZE
(Cone 10)

Frit #14 (O. Hommel)	90%
Kaolin	10
Chromium Oxide	5
	105%

This glaze can be used to give the "craters on the moon" effect. Other colorants can be used in place of the chromium.

#16 TRANSPARENT GLAZE
(Cone 5)

Feldspar	44%
Flint	24
Kaolin	2
Gerstley Borate (Colemanite)	20
Whiting	1
Zinc Oxide	3
Barium Carbonate	6
	100%

An excellent transparent glaze for this temperature. Any of the transparent colors listed below can be made opaque by the addition of 7% tin oxide. Colors are good but not unusual.

6.5%	Rutile for opaque cream
7.0%	Tin Oxide for white
3.0%	Copper Carbonate and 1% Rutile for emerald green
3.0%	Rutile and 0.25% Cobalt Oxide for opal blue
1.0%	Rutile, 2.5% Tin Vanadium Yellow Glaze Stain, and 0.25% Copper Carbonate for spring green
1.5%	Copper Oxide and 0.25% Cobalt Oxide for blue green
1.0%	Rutile and 5% Manganese Dioxide for amethyst

MC 532 TURQUOISE MATT
(Cone 5)

Barium Carbonate	25%
Nepheline Syenite	56
Ball Clay	6
Flint	7
Copper Carbonate	3
Lithium Carbonate	3
	100%

A beautiful copper blue matt; the copper may be omitted and other colorants used. Can be adapted for Cone 10 use by leaving out the lithium.

DARK ALBANY BROWN
(Cones 5-6)

Albany Slip Clay	83.8%
Cornwall Stone	3.2
Ball Clay	1.2
Flint	3.3
Whiting	1.1
Zinc Oxide	.6
Red Lead	6.8
	100.0%

This is a good transparent glossy glaze that may be used to make the bubbled "crater glazes." The G. S. Matt Glaze follows:

G. S. MATT GLAZE
(Cone 4 and up)

Nepheline Syenite	56%
Whiting	12
Zinc Oxide	11
Kaolin	19
Flint	2
	100%

This is a dry matt by itself, with good but limited results. It can be used effectively over the Dark Albany Brown Glaze for obtaining crater glazes.

GROUND GLASS GLAZE
(Cones 07-08)

Ground Glass or Cullet	27.3%
Frit #25 (O. Hommel)	27.3
White Lead	27.3
Kaolin	18.1
	100.0%

An excellent transparent glaze at Cone 08, this gives a thick, translucent effect at Cone 07. It works very well over underglazes. It can be made translucent for use at Cone 08 by the addition of 3% tin oxide. This glaze can be fired as high as Cone 10 oxidation if it is applied rather thinly. For colors, try:

1%	Cobalt Oxide for cobalt blue
2%	Copper Oxide for blue green
1%	Copper Carbonate for turquoise
5%	of any underglaze color should give excellent results at Cones 07-08

F. CARLTON BALL is a practicing potter, dedicated teacher, author and photographer. He has taught at the California College of Arts and Crafts, Oakland; the California School of Fine Arts, San Francisco; Mills College, Oakland; the University of Wisconsin, Madison; and Southern Illinois University, Carbondale. At present he is teaching at the University of Southern California at Los Angeles, where he is Professor of Fine Arts. In addition, he teaches ceramics at the College of Whittier and at the new Rio Hondo Junior College.

In spite of a heavy teaching schedule, Mr. Ball manages to find time to make and exhibit his own pottery, lecture and demonstrate, and experiment in almost every phase of ceramics. As an experimenter, he has explored the field of ceramic decoration in order to add interest, embellishment, and enrichment to his pottery forms. He is particularly concerned with textural effects and finds in nature the inspiration for many of his decorations. Carlton Ball is the co-author, with Janice Lovoos, of the book "Making Pottery Without a Wheel; Texture and Form in Clay," published in 1965 by Reinhold. Since 1953 Mr. Ball has been a regular contributor to *Ceramics Monthly Magazine* with articles on stoneware clay and glazes, throwing on the potter's wheel, and decoration. Some of the chapters in this handbook originally appeared in slightly different form in the pages of the magazine.